SCULPTURE

Kwele mask, 19th–20th century

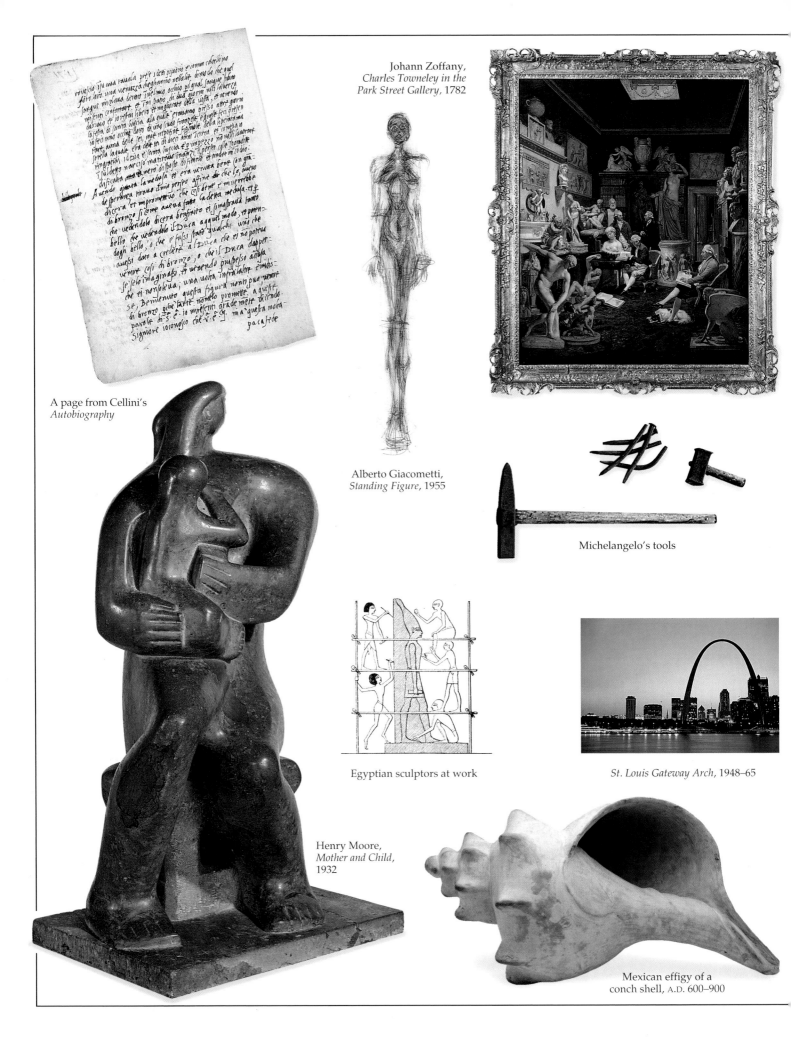

A page from Cellini's *Autobiography*

Johann Zoffany, *Charles Towneley in the Park Street Gallery*, 1782

Alberto Giacometti, *Standing Figure*, 1955

Michelangelo's tools

Egyptian sculptors at work

St. Louis Gateway Arch, 1948–65

Henry Moore, *Mother and Child*, 1932

Mexican effigy of a conch shell, A.D. 600–900

EYEWITNESS ART

SCULPTURE

MARY-JANE OPIE

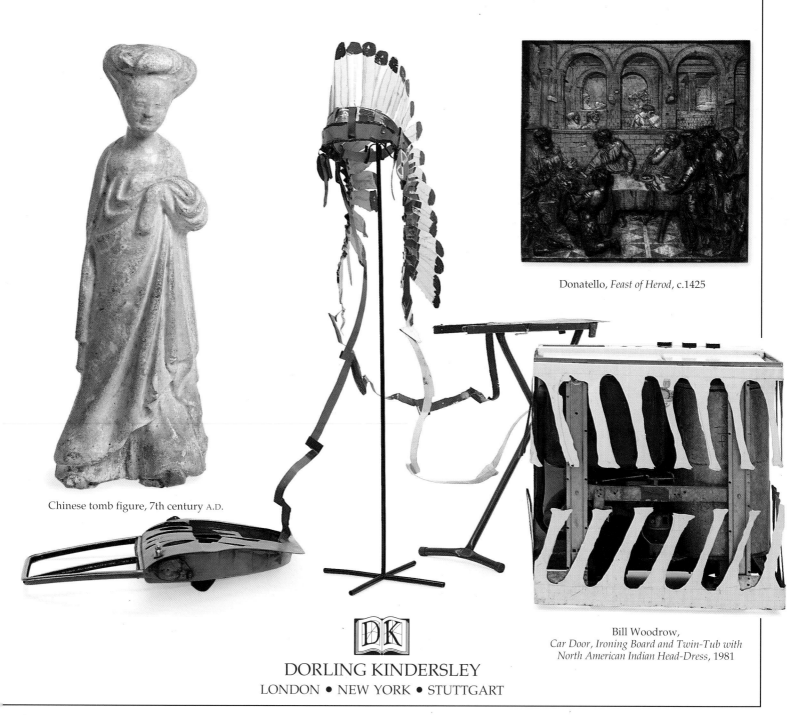

Donatello, *Feast of Herod*, c.1425

Chinese tomb figure, 7th century A.D.

Bill Woodrow,
*Car Door, Ironing Board and Twin-Tub with
North American Indian Head-Dress*, 1981

DK

DORLING KINDERSLEY

LONDON • NEW YORK • STUTTGART

Jacob Epstein,
Rock Drill, 1913–14

Edgar Degas,
Dancer, 1896–1911

Asante ritual figure,
late 19th century

A DORLING KINDERSLEY BOOK
To Dad and Mum

Editor Helen Castle
Art editor Liz Brown
Assistant editor Peter Jones
Design assistant Simon Murrell
Senior editor Gwen Edmonds
Managing editor Sean Moore
Managing art editor Toni Kay
U.S. editor Laaren Brown
Picture researchers Julia Harris-Voss,
Jo Evans
DTP designer Zirrinia Austin
Production controller Meryl Silbert

First American edition, 1994

2 4 6 8 10 9 7 5 3 1

Published in the United States by
Dorling Kindersley Publishing, Inc., 95 Madison Avenue,
New York, New York 10016

Library of Congress Cataloging-in-Publication Data
Opie, Mary-Jane.
Sculpture/Mary-Jane Opie. -- 1st American ed.
p.   cm.   -- (Eyewitness Art)
Includes index.
ISBN 1-56458-495-X
1. Sculpture – History. I. Title. II. Series.

NB60.064 1994   94-2593
730'.9--dc20   CIP
Color reproduction by GRB Editrice s.r.l.
Printed in Italy by A. Mondadori Editore, Verona

Gianlorenzo Bernini,
Apollo and Daphne,
1622–24

Mexican smiling face,
A.D. 600–900

*Group Attending
Crucifixion*, early
15th century

Contents

Egyptian marching hippopotamus, c.1880 B.C.

What is sculpture?

THE IMMEDIATE IMAGE that comes to mind for most of us when we think of a "great" sculpture is of a large three-dimensional figure in bronze or marble, standing on a plinth in a gallery – perhaps Michelangelo's *David* (p. 37) or Rodin's *Kiss* (p. 50). Sculpture, however, takes many forms. Though it is traditionally associated with the techniques of bronze casting (pp. 26–27), clay modeling (pp. 34–35), and wood- and marble carving (pp. 18–19 & 38–39), artists in the 20th century, such as Dan Flavin, have assembled pieces out of all sorts of industrial and everyday materials (see *Monument to V. Tatlin*, right). The idea that sculpture should be placed on display for solely artistic pleasure is a relatively recent one, limited to the West. Traditional non-Western art is often made for a particular use (see *Netsuke*, below) or its religious significance (*Figure of Ku*, left). Not always freestanding, sculpture can be found worldwide attached to buildings as architectural decoration (see *Demon and a Lady of Rank*, below).

FIGURE OF KU
*Hawaii; early 19th century;
3.5 ft (1.2 m) high; wood*
This statue represents Ku, the Hawaiian god of war, who was the most aggressive and active of the four cosmic deities traditionally worshiped by the people of the North Pacific islands. As a warrior god, Ku was particularly popular with the chiefs. This carving was originally positioned in an open-air temple.

NOK HEAD
*Nigeria; 5th century B.C.;
9¾ in (25 cm) high; terra-cotta*
This ancestor head was made by one of the earliest civilizations in West Africa, the Nok culture. Though it has the same flattened nose, pierced nostrils and eyes as others of its type, its facial expression is quite individual.

NETSUKE
*Japan; 18th century;
3 in (8 cm) high; ivory*
Sculpture can be both practical and ornamental. The Japanese have a long tradition of making sophisticated carvings on toggles, like this one, known as *netsuke*. They use them to attach pouches to cords that hang from their belts.

DEMON AND A LADY OF RANK
France; early 13th century; stone
Throughout history sculpture has been used to embellish buildings. The Mayans in ancient Mexico, for instance, adorned their pyramid-shaped temples with carved stone slabs (pp. 12–13). In Gothic cathedrals such as Chartres, sculptures were an integral part of the walls (pp. 30–31). The figures above decorate a porch.

APPENNINE
Giambologna; c.1570–80;
32¾ ft (10 m) high; rock, lava, and brick
Many sculptures remain in their original settings. This figure of a mountain god is part of a fountain in the gardens of the Medici Villa, which is situated in the foothills of the Appennine mountains in central Italy. Carved out of rock, *Appennine* appears like a volcano erupting out of the ground, secreting lava. His colossal body and muscular physique communicate his superhuman, divine status.

This plaster model was made by Canova's assistants

The construction is hung from this string

These strip lights depict a skyscraper

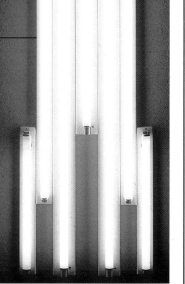

THREE GRACES
Antonio Canova; 1813; 65¾ in (167 cm) high; plaster
A sculptor's involvement in the production of a piece varies greatly. He, or she, may be responsible for the creation of an entire sculpture or just for its design. Although Antonio Canova (1757-1822) is said to be the artist of the *Three Graces*, he did not execute it. His assistants used this plaster replica to transfer the model that he had made into the marble figures, which they then carved (p. 47).

LINEAR CONSTRUCTION NO. 2
Naum Gabo; 1970–71; 4½ x 3¼ x 3¼ in
(11.5 x 8.5 x 8.5 cm); lucite and monofilament
The traditional sculptural techniques are subtractive and additive: carving is subtractive because it requires the sculptor to remove his material; modeling is additive because it means building up a work. In the 20th century, artists made a great departure and started constructing sculptures from various existing materials. Here, Naum Gabo (1890–1977) strung a basic frame with nylon thread to create different lines and planes.

MONUMENT FOR V. TATLIN
Dan Flavin; 1966–69; 12 x 2¼ x 3½ ft
(30.5 x 6 x 9 cm); light strips
Sculptors have always adapted new technologies to their needs. Even ancient methods and materials that we now consider traditional were once innovative. In the 20th century, sculptors have consciously employed new media to keep in step with their viewers. Dan Flavin uses 20th-century lighting systems to refer to modern styles of living. This piece is a tribute to the Russian architect and painter Vladimir Tatlin (1885–1953), who designed some of the first skyscrapers.

Stone Age forms

IN SPITE OF ITS ASSOCIATION WITH EARLY MAN, the Stone Age cannot be isolated to a particular period in history. The term describes any age previous to the discovery of metal, when stone was the predominant material. Although its starting date is pinpointed at 30,000 B.C., a few cultures have been labeled as Stone Age as late as the 20th century. Stone Age sculptures are made from stone, bone, wood, and clay. Often lacking in detail, they were, until recently, dismissed as "primitive." Representing the struggle for survival, works depict animals – the suppliers of food, fuel, and clothing – and fertility symbols, which ensure the continued existence of the tribe. Along with small-scale pieces, a few permanent structures have also been built (see below).

STONEHENGE
Salisbury Plain, Britain; c.2100–2000 B.C.; diameter: 118¼ ft (c.36 m); stone
Shrouded in mystery, this structure is traditionally linked to pagan midsummer festivities. Seemingly primitive in construction, the stones are, in fact, held in place with carved joints; the horizontal beams are leveled and the uprights shaped – when viewed from beneath, the sides do not appear to converge. The present monument is not the result of a single building effort, but of several remodelings during the English Stone Age.

MAMMOTH

France; 1300 B.C.;
3½ in (9 cm); bone and antler ivory
Before the Ice Age, mammoths were a common source of food. Through this carving, the sculptor paid his respects to his prey. Although highly stylized – the tusks are carved in relief – the animal's massive bulk is given life by its raised trunk and tail.

There has been much speculation as to how these sandstones were transported to Salisbury Plain from the Marlborough Downs, 20 miles away

CANDELABRA

Peru; 800 B.C.–A.D. 600; field-size; sand
Massive land sculptures, like this, remain an enigma. Visible only from a distance, their creators could never have seen them. There has been much speculation as to their purpose. It has even been suggested that they were created as messages to the gods or extraterrestrials. The position of this candelabra, or cactus, overlooking the Pacific Ocean, at Paracras in Peru, suggests that it was used to navigate ships. Although it is pre-Inca, we cannot be certain which culture made it. However, the Chacín people, in the north, used cacti as symbols of power.

FEMALE IDOL WITH ARMS FOLDED

Greece; 2700–2300 B.C.; 8½ in (22 cm) high; marble
Though the early Greek Cycladic culture used bronze tools by the third century B.C., their only notable sculptures – figures such as this – were produced with Stone Age techniques. This statuette would have been carved with a hard volcanic rock and rubbed down with emery (p. 62). Originally painted, these figures were not intended to appear so geometrical. Theories as to the statuettes' use vary from escorts for the dead to substitutes for sacrifice.

BISON

France; c.15,000 B.C.; 24 x 25 in (61 x 63.5 cm); clay
These clay bison are situated in the chamber of a cave 750 yards (700 m) from its entrance in Tuc d'Audoubert, southern France. Devoid of all superfluous detail, their fluid bodies are convincing in their proportions and movement. They are made of clay – a brittle material – and were probably part of a larger group, of which only two pairs remain. In both, a male bison follows a female. This seems to suggest that their original significance was associated with the magic of fertility rites.

9

"Tribal" objects

MANY SCULPTURES MADE BY traditional non-Western cultures can be seen in Western museums and galleries. Often in glass cases, they are now displayed in an alien context. These works, which were never intended to be art objects alone, cannot be appreciated solely for their visual appearance. The form that the sculptures take was principally determined by the purpose for which they were produced and the materials available locally. All three Inuit (Eskimo) objects on the opposite page are carved out of walrus ivory, which is abundant in the Arctic. There are also other less obvious considerations of lifestyle and religious beliefs. Nomadic hunting groups, like the Inuit and the interior peoples of North America, had to make their art objects small and highly portable. This was because the itinerant nature of their lives – following herds of prey across vast tracts of land – made it impossible for them to carry heavy or bulky items. The *Polar Bear* ivory charm (right), for instance, was small enough to fit in an Inuit's pocket.

NECK PENDANT
Maori; 18th century;
3 in (7.5 cm) high; nephrite
Pendants were worn as ornaments by both Maori men and women. Carved from many different materials, they depicted stylized figures. This translucent nephrite stone (p. 62), which is only four millimeters thick, has holes carved into its surface to bring the figure to life by increasing the play of light.

BABY CARRIER
Kenyah or Kayan; 19th–20th century;
17½ x 14 in (35.5 x 44.5 cm); wood and shell
The form and decoration of this baby carrier from Borneo are symbolic of its protective function. The backrest encases the child like a cocooning shield, and the carvings of the white-eyed figures and the dog-dragon guard the young occupant against evil spirits. Carved in two parts, the individual pieces are held together with tight-fitting lugs and pins. The heavy hardwood and intricately carved decoration suggest that it was used by a person of high rank on special occasions.

LADLE

Wishram or Wasco;
19th century; 6½ in (16.5 cm) long; wood

From the Columbia River region of North America, this ladle is simple and solid in form. Its only decoration is the handle, which is carved as a wolflike figure with a second human head in place of a tail. Carved with its purpose foremost in mind, the ladle has a groove running its length, to keep it from dripping. It has darkened with constant use and fish oil.

The main head of this mythical animal is wolflike

IVORY HEAD

Inuit; 19th century;
1¼ in (3 cm) high; walrus ivory and beads

As the end of a drum handle, this head was originally attached at the back to a drum's circular frame. With its colored bead eyes and delicately carved features, it shows the intricacy of Inuit work. Drums were used by the Inuit to accompany rituals and dances.

POLAR BEAR

Inuit; c.1½ in (4 cm); ivory

It is probable that this was a charm, carried by an Inuit shaman (holy man). Here, the balance between man and his prey – necessary for long-term hunting – is emphasized by the fact that a man is depicted riding on a polar bear's back.

THE INUIT ON THE MOVE

Traditionally, the Inuit relied entirely on animals for their subsistence: their diet consisted almost wholly of raw meat; their clothes were made out of fur and leather; and animal fat was used to make oil for their lamps. To hunt, the Inuit had to be always on the move, making long expeditions from their coastal and inland base camps. To move across the tundra, they sometimes rode on sleds pulled by huskies.

DRILL BOW

Inuit; 19th century;
13½ in (34.5 cm) long; walrus ivory and hide

The drill was one of the most important Inuit tools. Used like a stone-cutting drill (p. 38), it cut slabs of ice for shelters or pierced through frozen surfaces for fishing and hunting. The hide, twisted around the vertical shaft, drew horizontally back and forth, rotating the drill. The large, flat ivory bow, which usually depicted hunting scenes, formed an ideal surface for engraving. Here, it shows a herd of caribou, grazing, resting, and running into the firing line of Inuit hunters. For emphasis, the incised lines were filled with black and red pigment.

Here, a pair of caribou are shown grazing peacefully, unaware of the presence of Inuit hunters

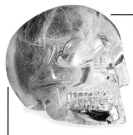

CRYSTAL SKULL
Though Mesoamerican culture was oppressed by the Spanish after the conquest of 1519, it still survived. This skull was made by native Mexicans with the aid of a European jeweler's wheel.

Ancient Mesoamerica

THE ARTS OF PRECOLUMBIAN Mexico and Guatemala (c.2000 B.C.–A.D.1519) are not the product of a single evolving culture, but of several civilizations – including the Olmecs, Mayas, Toltecs, and Aztecs – that coexisted and succeeded one another. In spite of their diversity, most sculptures were symbolic, closely associated with religious beliefs and rituals. Their exact meaning can now only be guessed at; the societies that produced them had no written records. Though stone sculptures were used on a large scale in architectural settings (see *Uxmal*, right), they were carved with basic stone tools, as metal came late to Mexico. A strong ceramic tradition meant that many items were made out of clay.

MINIATURE STELE
Maya; height: 19½ in (49.5 cm); limestone
The upright stone slab, or stele, was one of the most important formats used by the Maya during the Classic period (C.A.D. 200–600). Mounted in open squares between buildings, they were erected to commemorate the passing of time and the ascension of new religious rulers. Cut in low relief with elaborate, curvilinear patterns, they were incised with stone tools.

THE SMILING FACE
Veracruz culture;
A.D. 600–900; height: 6½ in (15.8 cm); buff earthenware
One of many sculptures made from a single mold, this "smiling face," with its triangular head, patterned headdress, oval eyes, and smiling mouth, is a good example of its type. Discovered in ancient Maya burial sites near Veracruz, such smiling faces are occasionally found as part of whole figures. It is thought that all the heads originally had bodies, but were ritually decapitated before their burial.

The surface of the shell is coated with white slip

CONCH SHELL
Maya?; A.D. 300–900; height: 8½ in (22 cm); earthenware and white slip
Discovered in architectural caches and burial sites, conch shells were produced as offerings to the gods. Little is known about this particular shell from Guatemala, which is made out of clay and coated in white slip (p. 62).

TURQUOISE MASK

Aztec; c.1500; 6½ in (17 cm); turquoise, wood, and pearl shell

By the 15th century, the Aztecs had imposed their power on many of the Mesoamerican cultures. This sacred mask was made by a Mixtec artisan. Well known as the best craftsmen, the Mixtec group supplied the Aztec rulers with their most exquisite objects. The mother-of-pearl eyes and mouth of this mask endow it with a lifelike quality. It is covered in turquoise – one of the most precious materials – which was used to symbolize water, day, and sky.

THE NUNNERY, UXMAL

The structures of Uxmal are complemented by large architectural sculptures. Geometric assemblies of serpent-mask mosaic forms decorate the upper confines of the buildings.

CHACMOOL

Toltec; A.D.1300–1519; 3 x 5 ft (91.5 x 152.5 cm); stone and polychrome

Found at many of the later Mexican sites, Chacmool figures were meant to mediate between the gods and man by holding out sacrificial offerings. (Human sacrifice was an important part of many Mesoamerican religions.) Like all the original works, this Chacmool is brightly colored.

PYRAMID OF MAGICIAN, UXMAL

Uxmal is the best preserved of all Maya sites. Built between A.D. 600–1000 in Yucatán, Mexico, as a city governed by religious leaders, it is dominated by this ninety-foot-high sanctuary. A five-layer structure, it was built over two earlier temples. The smooth sides were plastered and painted with subjects that inspired divine devotion and honored the city's dignitaries. The massive stairway ascends to two different types of doorway styled as a schematic mask of Chac, the rain god.

Rituals and ancestors

CROWN
Just as ancestor worship ensured the survival of chiefdoms, royal regalia emphasized a chief's position. This crown, made for a Dogon chief, was skillfully cast in brass, a rare metal in Mali.

TRADITIONAL AFRICAN ART IS extremely diverse. It derives from a whole continent of cultures. Although the sculptures shown here come only from central and western Africa, they range from classical Benin bronzes (far right) to the simplified shapes of the Kwele mask and the Asante ritual figure (below). In order to fully appreciate and understand an object, it is necessary to know where it originated from and the beliefs that surrounded it there. These sculptures were all produced for their use in rituals and ancestor worship. For instance, the Benin head of an oba (right) was displayed on a royal altar, where sacrifices were made to it. In the West, people have tended to trace the style and form of African sculptures to their area of origin rather than to the individuals who made them. However, this does not mean that sculptors are not well known or respected within their communities. In Africa, the traditional techniques of woodcarving and bronze casting are highly developed.

HEAD
Fang; 19th–20th century; 13½ in (26 cm); wood
Concentrating on the head – the seat of the soul – this elegant figure with piercing eyes stands guardian over the relics of ancestors. Its power was recharged by ritual anointing.

MASK
Kwele; 19th–20th century; 11 in (28 cm); wood
This is similar to a famous mask owned by the French painter André Derain (1880–1954). It is carved simply with the use of an adze and painted with kaolin, a white clay. The white face suggests that it was produced for an ancestors' cult, common in the Congo, where it was made. Almost flat, made out of a soft wood, it could possibly have been hung rather than worn.

RITUAL FIGURE
Asante; 19th century; 10 in (25 cm) high; wood
This type of figure is made by the Asante of Ghana. With its flat, round head, it represents the Asante ideal of beauty. Pregnant Asante women carry these figures in the hope that they will make their babies beautiful. They are meant to obtain magical powers from wood, a living material.

DIVINATION CUP
Yoruba; 19th century; 9½ in (24 cm) high; wood
A Yoruba diviner in southern Nigeria would have used this cup to hold the 16 palm nuts with which he cast the Ifa oracle – the prophecies at the center of Yoruba religion. Yoruba individuals, cult groups, and rulers consult the Ifa system of divination – never daring to go against its advice.

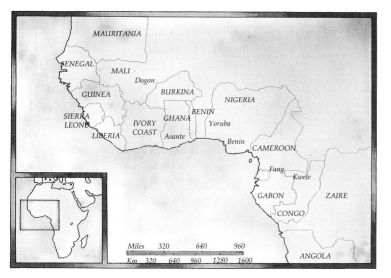

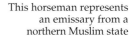

This horseman represents an emissary from a northern Muslim state

HORSEMAN
Benin; 18th century;
23½ in (60 cm) high; brass
In Benin, brass casting using the lost-wax process (pp. 26–27) was a royal prerogative: the craftsmen were the servants of the king and were forced to observe strict palace rituals. This horseman is cruder and less realistic than the earlier bronzes shown below.

WHERE ARE THESE AFRICAN SCULPTURES FROM?
The works illustrated here come from a comparatively small part of the entire African continent. They originated in cultural regions in western and central Africa. Many of these areas were originally governed as kingdoms and have the strongest traditions of rituals and ancestor worship. Probably the most precious and collected African sculptures, in the West, are those from the old kingdom of Benin, in west Africa (see this page). One of the most powerful African states, Benin resisted direct colonial domination until the end of the 19th century. Much of its art was made as furniture for altars, dedicated to the royal ancestor cult, onto which blood was dripped from animal and human sacrifices. In 1897, the British used human sacrifice as an excuse to enter Benin and carry out their own massacre of the Bini. In Europe, Benin City became notorious, known as "the city of blood."

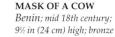

MASK OF A COW
Benin; mid 18th century;
9½ in (24 cm) high; bronze
Based on fluid, curving lines, this mask is technically advanced. The horns must have been cast whole as they are complete at the back. However, the real expertise is displayed in the more fragile areas, where there are sophisticated systems of support. The ears, which were made like large leaves to cover the holes for suspending the mask, have a framework of "veins" or integral rods. The face is patterned with arabesques and stylized marks. It is probable that the mask was originally hung from the back of an altar screen.

HEAD OF AN OBA
Benin; early 16th century; 9 in (23 cm) high; brass and iron
This representation of an oba (king) is one of a group of about ten heads made for a single funeral. Possibly the first batch of altar heads ever to have been made, these portraits have, in retrospect, been considered the finest Benin sculptures. Produced during the early period of Benin art, they are perhaps the most exquisite lost-wax castings ever made anywhere. Their thickness varies from only one to three millimeters, and they are evenly and beautifully finished. This head would have been the work of a number of craftsmen. It is the generalized ideal of what a tribal elder should look like rather than an individual portrait. The double line of the eyelids, broad nose, and full lips are a sort of stylized shorthand used to describe the features.

Eastern deities

SINCE ANCIENT TIMES, Buddhism has been the main impetus behind Asian art. The religious teachings of the Buddha (c.563–480 B.C.), who came from northeast India, were spread by missionaries throughout Asia via the the silk routes that carried Chinese silks to the West. Buddhism penetrated China during the Han Dynasty (206 B.C.–A.D. 220), Korea in the 4th century A.D., and Japan during the 6th century A.D. The success of this new faith and its art was due to the fact that it was able to live alongside, and even merge with, older belief systems such as Hinduism in India, Confucianism in China, and Shinto in Japan. Though Indian artists worked in separate Hindu and Buddhist communities, their art was not stylistically distinguishable. The various deities they depicted could only be identified by the form and attributes they carried. In Japan, artists were affiliated to temple workshops, and in China, craftsmen were attached to the imperial court.

IMPERIAL PALACE
Peking, China; begun 1403
In China, a variety of workshops existed in the vicinity of the "forbidden city," where items were made for the court and for the emperor to give as gifts. Many of these works of art were given to temples to legitimize the rule of the emperor as the Son of Heaven.

TOMB FIGURE
China; 7th century A.D.;
11 in (28 cm) high; glazed earthenware
Statuettes such as this were buried in tombs to care and protect the deceased in the afterlife. During the 7th century, China was open to the outside world – foreign influences and goods were brought back to China along the trade routes. By depicting the religious and social customs of the period, tomb figures offer an unrivaled insight into Chinese life. This lady's costume and dressed hair, for instance, illustrate contemporary fashion.

SACRED GENERAL
Japan; 1573–1614; lacquered wood
This is one of 12 sacred generals made to guard the Buddhist temple of To-ji, in Kyoto, Japan. Depicted as a warrior, stabbing at demons beneath his feet, the general illustrates one of the more ferocious stylistic periods in Japanese art.

TERRA-COTTA ARMY
China; 210 B.C.; life-size; terra-cotta
This 7,000-strong terra-cotta army was made for the tomb of the first emperor, Quin Shi Huang Di, to defend his spirit in the afterlife. Part cast, part modeled, the head and hands of each life-size figure were made individually, then painted to distinguish character and rank. The figures are portraits, depicting individuals rather than formulaic types. Of the 7,000, no two faces are the same.

SHIVA NATARAJA
Chola, India; 11th–12th century; 32¼ in (82 cm) high; bronze
This perfectly composed ceremonial work exemplifies the ideal of inner consciousness and emotion. As Lord of the Dance and the Hindu god of creation and destruction, the Shiva is a study of motion and vibration, expressing the power of the cosmos and the universal flux of energy. Flames of rebirth and annihilation swirl around the calm central face. The long hair represents asceticism, while the lifted foot shows detachment from materialism. Although gods were depicted as having a human form, their proportions, poses, and gestures were based on the strict metaphysical rules of ancient religion.

BUDDHA
This Buddha from Borobudur (see below) presents an image of timeless equilibrium amid earthly chaos. Initially covered in plaster and then painted, its smooth surface creates a clear silhouette: in the strong Asian light, surface details disappear.

The Buddha's shape is echoed by the surrounding domes

A demon lies crushed under the right foot of the dancing Shiva

BOROBUDUR
Central Java, Indonesia; completed c.A.D. 840; 360 x 115 ft (100 x 35 m)
Borobudur, the man-made "mountain of Buddhas," was created to illustrate Buddha's life and teachings. Each of the 72 domed stupas (Buddhist temples) contains a statue of the Buddha to teach and inspire pilgrims through the various stages of enlightenment, from mortal man to the divine serenity of Buddha. Ten miles of carved reliefs, which read from left to right, ascend the structure, comprising full figures, pictorial representations, and writings. Built with a solid core of rubble, the highly carved volcanic ashlar stones are fixed with mortar.

Carving a totem pole

THE TOTEM POLE is the most monumental form of woodcarving. Traditionally made by the tribal groups of the Pacific Northwest – the Tsimshian, Haida, Kwakiutl, Tlingit, Bella Coola, and Nootka – they were carved in an area of dense forestation that extended from Alaska to the state of Washington. Adept at all kinds of wood-working, these Native Americans used wood to make everything from masks to houses. Though totem poles existed before European contact, the introduction of steel tools in the 19th century made wood carving easier, and carvers became more skilled. Totem poles varied in height from nine to ninety feet and were made from the trunk of a cedar tree. Complex in design, they depicted animals and beings, commemorating ancestral myths (see *Hole in the Sky*, below). Expensive to produce, requiring the payment of skilled carvers, they were a deliberate display of wealth and privilege.

RED CEDAR
Though cedar, fir, spruce, and hemlock are the most common trees in the Pacific Northwest, the red cedar is the most suitable for totem poles. Red cedar grows up to 200 feet tall, the wood splits straight and cleanly, and it is more resistant to decay than most other woods.

Forest and mountain animals, such as the wolf, were generally depicted in a crouched, seated position

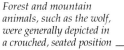

Totem poles were positioned in front of family houses

The dense forest of the Northwest can be seen in the background

LONG HUTS AND BEACH
This photograph of a Tsimshian village shows how totem poles were placed like prestigious signs outside a particular family's house. Though houses and totem poles were permanent, their makers were migratory, occupying their plank houses only in the winter. In summer, they followed their main food source, the salmon, upriver. Carving was confined to the long winters.

HOLE IN THE SKY
Every pole is a visual record of the mythical stories that traced a family's ancestral lines. These were proclaimed in full only during official ceremonies that were held to celebrate the completion of a totem pole. A pole's design generally fuses crests, ancestor figures, mythical and semihistorical events together. Here, the wolf features most prominently; he is the principal crest of the pole's owner. All the animal images are rendered in a symmetrical and angular manner. The wolf appears in a seated, compressed position, while the other creatures are shown from above with their limbs and tails pinned out at their sides.

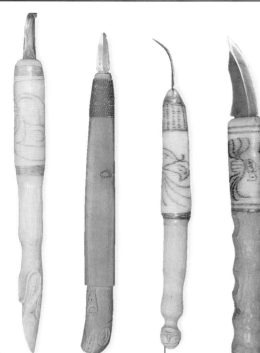

Carvers used a variety
of curved knives

TOOLS
A number of tools were used by the traditional
Northwest carver. The most essential of these were
the elbow adze, the D-adze, and the curved knife. A
carver generally picked up an elbow adze to hew his
first rough forms out of a log. A D-adze was either
employed like a chisel, to give a carving definition, or
its blade was dragged lengthwise over the wood to
create a rippling finish. The prominent, deeply cut
details, which characterize the totem pole, were
obtained with the aid of the curved knife.

The first
rough forms
of the totem
were hewn
out with the
elbow adze

*The head of a figure is
carved into this handle*

The D-shaped
adze, used length-
wise, creates a
rippling finish

*The blade is tied to
the adze with string*

WORKING ON A TOTEM POLE
All totem poles have a definite front and back. By placing the tree trunk
horizontally on its side, the carvers leave the reverse side blank. They work
up the pole, at every stage, from the bottom to the top. First they peel the
bark off, and then they chop away the sapwood. When the pole is cleaned, a
design is drawn on with charcoal. (A model is also often made as a guide to
the carvers.) Outline cuts are incised all along the pole with a D-adze and a
knife to separate the different shapes. Next, the details of each animal are
more closely defined, using a D-adze, knife, and, occasionally, a hammer.
Throughout the process, the wood is kept malleable with pans of hot water.

*Here, one of the carvers
is using an elbow adze*

*Another elbow adze is
positioned ready for use*

*A model is placed beside the
totem pole to guide the carvers*

Ancient Egypt

No OTHER CIVILIZATION has a cultural history that has remained so constant to one style for such a vast period of time (3168–332 B.C.). Egyptian art may at first seem naive, unnecessarily bound by conventions of form and subject matter, and immune to the social upheavals and changes of power that shaped the dynasties of the pharaohs. However, sculpture was not subject to artistic whim, but produced to illustrate religious ideals and to decorate temples, which explains the lack of any abrupt artistic changes. Initially, sculptural forms were based on the solid geometric proportions of the surface of a building (see the *Temple of Ramesses*, below); later, however, when pieces became freestanding, they remained true to these rules (see *Standing Couple*, right). As all artistic activities were inspired by the gods, it is difficult, if not impossible, to separate religious and secular works – many sculptors were priests; they created sculptures that followed religious formulas, inherited from previous generations. Once completed, the artworks underwent a religious rite – "opening of the mouth"– that charged an inanimate, man-made object with a divine spirit.

CAT
c.700-600 B.C.; 13 x 10 in (33 x 25 cm); bronze
The head and the decorative pendant are the only distinguishing features of this cat. Stylized and strictly symmetrical, it is a harmonious combination of anatomy and design. Found in large numbers, this type of sculpture contained animal remains and was presented in the temples as offerings to the cat goddess, Bastet.

TEMPLE OF RAMESSES II
Built in c.1257 B.C., this mortuary temple, cut deep into the sandstone cliffs at Abu Simbel, has a traditional inward-looking plan of interior courts and many-columned halls. Hewn from the same rock, the facade is treated as a vast gateway. The doorway is flanked by four 60-foot-high, seated figures of Ramesses with smaller figures of his family standing between the legs. The broad surfaces and monumental appearance of these statues are contrived to assert the Pharaoh's absolute power.

MARCHING HIPPOPOTAMUS
c.1880 B.C.; 7¼ in (18.5 cm) length; faience
Popular as offerings to gods, animal sculptures were often made of stone or, as here, faience, a decorated earthenware; the scarcity of wood in Egypt's arid climate made it precious, reserved for important pieces. An enemy of the Egyptian gods, the hippo was regarded as an evil omen.

The hippo's plump body is described by simple, round forms

THE GIZA SPHINX
c. 2650 B.C; stone
Representing the power of the reigning Pharaoh, Khephren, the Sphinx combines the tense, latently destructive power of a lion's body with the benevolent power of a ruler and god. The sphinx at Giza is carved from a single rock, found in a quarry near the king's temple, and has a monumental calm. It stands as a terrifying guardian of the pyramids and the Nile valley, linking the Pharaoh to his supposed father, the sun god, Ra.

TOOLS

So little has changed in the methods of stone carving that an ancient Egyptian sculptor could easily identify and use 20th-century tools. Their drills, punches, chisels, and abrasives are similar in design to those still used today.

This clipping chisel removed small amounts of stone

Sculptors created smooth grooves with this rubbing stone

The drill bow was used by the Inuit (p. 11) and by Renaissance sculptors (p.38)

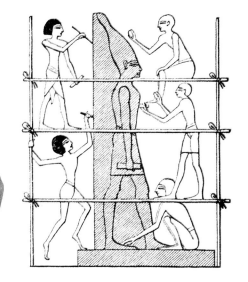

EGYPTIAN SCULPTORS AT WORK

Using chisels made of hard stone, craftsmen roughly blocked out the figure. Gently rubbing the surface with sand or pumice stones, sculptors created fine details and polished surfaces. Breakages were reattached with sophisticated jointing systems. The profession of individual sculptor did not exist in ancient Egypt – instead workshops arose, where stonemasons, carpenters and jewelers worked together, overseen by a designer-cum-sculptor. So important was this job that it was reserved for high priests and members of the royal family. The skill of the craftsmen lay not in reproducing the world around them, but in representing the ideal world of the afterlife.

SEATED SCRIBE
c.2620–2350 B.C.; 21¼ x 17¼ x 13¼ in (54 x 44 x 35 cm); painted limestone

In a society where the masses were illiterate, members of the ruling family were sometimes portrayed as scribes. This upright figure retains the quality of a sculpture attached to a building.

The scribe's stomach has fatty folds that symbolize his status as a well-fed man with an "office" job

STANDING COUPLE
c.2500–2350 B.C.; 21 x 8½ in (53 x 21.5 cm); painted limestone

For the first time in sculpture, a woman is shown not as a fertility object or a goddess, but as the equal of a man, guiding her husband forward. The figures are painted in the traditional colors: red for men and the outdoor life, yellow for women and indoor occupation. A slow change in sculptural styles and innovations meant that practical conventions of previous eras still persisted. The upright stance, the blocked-in areas between body and legs, and the forward step all refer back to the time when sculptures were bonded to a building and were made of more delicate materials – papyrus reeds and clay – that needed greater support. The woman's left arm and the man's left leg, however, stand out independently of the main structure.

Heroic Greek art

THE MONUMENTAL PERIOD of ancient Greek sculpture is often regarded as the starting point of Western art. Spanning more than five hundred years (c.660–150 B.C.), it originated with the modeling of rudimentary forms and developed into a highly skilled and realistic art. One of its most important innovations was the evolution of the human figure, as illustrated below. The earliest statues – such as the *Kouros* (below left) – were produced after Greece's expansion into Egypt and were strongly influenced by Egyptian art. Simple in execution, they were all that was possible with copper tools and soft stones. It was the Greeks' subsequent perfection of techniques including marble carving and bronze casting that allowed them to create a more realistic and, in turn, heroic interpretation of the human form, such as the *Discus Thrower* (below right).

PARTHENON
Originally highly decorated, the Parthenon was painted in primary colors and embellished with gold. It was built as a temple between 447 and 432 B.C. and dedicated to the goddess Athena. Iktinos is believed to have been the architect and Pheidas the sculptor. Sited on the Acropolis, above Athens, the Parthenon is the focal point of the city.

KRITIAN BOY
Kritios; c. 490 B.C.;
33¼ in (86 cm) high; marble
This figure departs from the stiff frontal pose of the *Kouros*. The flexed right leg and lowered right hip create a relaxed, slight S-curve.

The physical and facial features of the athlete are idealized

The figure takes on the form of its marble block

This kouros is tentatively carved, as if it were a relief

KOUROS
c.530 B.C; 6¼ ft
(1.91 m) high; marble
Kouroi, like this one, were carved to decorate sanctuaries of the gods. Sculpted in a geometric style, they were influenced by Egyptian sculpture. Physical features, such as knees and wigs, are formulaic approximations of what they depict, rather than observations from real life.

Weight is borne entirely on the left leg

DISCUS THROWER
Roman copy; original 450 B.C.;
49¼ in (125 cm) high; marble
This is one of many Roman copies made from a Greek original, now lost. It is, however, the only one with its head in the correct position. Here, the stiffness and symmetry of earlier sculptures are replaced by the rhythmic contrasts of the human figure: hips and shoulders slant; the body twists; and one arm counterbalances the other. Although the figure appears realistic, its perfectly proportioned features suggest that it is an idealized portrait of a young athlete.

THE PARTHENON FRIEZE
447–432 B.C.; 43 in (109 cm) high; marble
Before their removal by the British, the Parthenon reliefs encircled the entire temple. They formed a continuous frieze, depicting the Panathenaea Procession in honor of Athena. No two faces or poses portrayed appear the same – each individual is shown to be intent on his own action. The overlapping horses provide the linear format of the frieze with a sense of movement and rhythm, while also creating a convincing sense of space and depth within the relief.

HEAD OF SOPHOCLES
c.400 B.C.; 12½ in (32 cm) high; bronze
Until the fifth century B.C., portraits were identified by age, dress, or inscription. The development of bronze casting by two sculptors on the island of Samos in c.570 B.C., however, freed sculpture from the restrictions of more brittle materials, such as stone. This encouraged sculptors to explore the movement of the figure and to evolve the notion of portraiture as the realistic depiction of the sitter.

CARYATID
420 B.C.; 7½ ft (2.31 m); marble
This caryatid – a column in the form of a draped female figure – was originally one of six that supported the porch of the Erechtheum, a small temple that shares the Acropolis with the Parthenon. The overall shape and static pose of the caryatid give it the appearance of a Corinthian column, while the arrangement of the robes suggests a more graceful feminine form beneath. The drapery provides grooves and planes for light and shade to play across, creating rhythm and tension within the figure.

MAP OF GREECE IN ALEXANDER'S TIME
Greek sculpture was greatly influenced by other foreign cultures that came under the umbrella of the Greek empire. This map shows the full extent of Greek imperialism. In 334 B.C., Alexander the Great invaded Persia, only to press on through Asia Minor, and then south and east to Egypt, Afghanistan, and India.

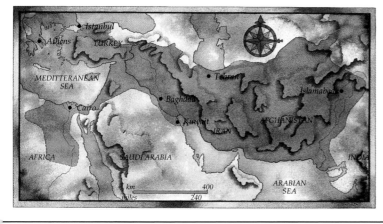

Imperial Rome

AS BRILLIANT ENGINEERS, architects, and politicians, the Romans can be credited with shaping the landscape of Europe. Their art history, however, is rarely presented in such glorious terms. In 750 B.C., the Greeks colonized southern Italy, imposing on it their civilization and cultural ideals. Italian artists adopted the techniques, styles, and subjects of their conquerors – often copying directly from Greek originals. When the city of Rome expanded in the second to third century B.C., it became the center of an empire. Imitations of Greek art were subordinated to the Roman ideals of symmetry and proportion, while a sense of naturalism was inherited from the earlier culture of the native Etruscans.

By the beginning of the first century A.D., the Romans' conquest of surviving Hellenistic kingdoms made Rome a hub of artistic activity. Realism rapidly replaced idealization and hero worship as portraits became a truthful reflection of their subjects. Today, surviving private commissions and triumphal monuments glorifying military victories convey a vivid picture of Roman life.

CLAUDIUS PORTRAIT
A.D. 41–51; life-size; marble
In contrast to their idealized Greek predecessors, Roman busts were realistic, showing "warts and all." They were usually colored – painted and gilded.

MOURNING WOMAN
c.A.D. 100; 70 in (178 cm) high; marble
Beautiful female forms such as this were carved en masse. The head, commissioned by the buyer, was made separately and added later. Here, a veil hides the join and provides a dark background to make the facial features stand out.

AUGUSTUS
Early 1st century A.D.; 80 in (203 cm) high; marble
While the Greeks portrayed their heroes as philosophers or idealists, the Romans were depicted as men of action. This is an official portrait of the Emperor Augustus, a confident superhuman, addressing his army. The whole piece is loaded with allegorical meaning. On the armor are reliefs of classical myths, and a cupid and dolphin support his right leg, recalling Augustus's mythical descent from Aeneas. Painted in bright colors and gilded, the statue was intended to constantly remind Roman subjects of this Caesar's divine and imperial heritage.

LAOCOÖN
c.A.D. 30; 8 ft (2.5 m) high; marble
When the *Laocoön* was rediscovered in Rome, in 1506, it became one of the most influential classical works: Michelangelo hailed it as "a singular miracle." It was believed to be either an original Greek work or a Roman replica of one. Less accomplished than Greek masterpieces, however, its figures lack a coherent scale, its triangular composition is poorly balanced, and the snake is biting like a dog.

TRAJAN'S COLUMN

A.D. 106–13; 108¼ ft (33 m) diameter x 3.85 m (32 ft) high; marble

The reliefs on Trajan's Column are some of the finest in Roman art. They read like a 50-yard-long comic strip that spirals around the column, telling the story of the Emperor Trajan's two victorious campaigns against Dacia (now Romania). To fit such a complicated narrative into a narrow strip, the sculptors devised various tricks of symbolism and perspective. "Ancient" perspective, multiple vanishing points, and bird's-eye views are all employed. The reliefs were not intended to be seen in their present setting, here, in Trajan's Forum in Rome. The column originally stood in a courtyard surrounded by galleries, where the intricacies of the various levels of the once brightly colored reliefs could be examined.

THE COMIC STRIP

With the action reading left to right, the winning army, Trajan's or Dacian's, is always advancing up the column. Symbolism allows 12 soldiers to represent a thousand, a few bodies a massacre. As shown here, separate episodes overlap on a strip approximately three feet wide. At the bottom, an army appears to be traveling by boat, while above, officials gather. Trajan, who is the largest figure, takes the starring role in this and every scene.

COLUMN DETAIL

Densely packed, the strip conveys a strong sense of action. Even here, where the armies are not shown in combat, they appear in frenzied preparation. Throughout, drapery binds the figures and narrative together, often billowing in a single direction.

THE BRONZE HORSES OF ST. MARK'S, VENICE

c.A.D. 300; 91¾ x 29 x 99½ in (233 x 74 x 253 cm); metal alloy

These four magnificent horses signal the transition from Roman to Byzantine art. Originally made for the Hippodrome (a horse stadium) – one of the grandest of Emperor Constantine's buildings, in Constantinople – they became a symbol of imperial power in the East. (In 1204, Venice plundered them and placed them on display in the center of the city). Individually cast, each horse has a strongly stylized mane and ears. Though lacking in anatomical detail, the muscles, skin, and hair are accurately observed. They are made from a mix of copper, silver, and gold.

Bronze casting

THE ABILITY TO CREATE fine but enduring sculptures has challenged artists for centuries. Bronze, an alloy of copper and tin, is one of the strongest materials, but is difficult to work. Artists have tried manipulating the metal when it is molten and hammering it when cold. Casting, the most successful method, first emerged in the Bronze Age, when hollow stones were filled with molten bronze. The ancient Egyptians (pp. 20–21) cast on a small scale, making larger pieces out of solid sections. It was the Greeks (pp. 22–23) who perfected the lost-wax process (below and right) and were able to produce large statues with unsupported limbs and delicate details (right). Though casting developed separately in Africa (p. 15) and elsewhere, in the Western world it became synonymous with classical art.

THE PIREUS APOLLO
520 B.C.; 6¼ ft (1.9 m); bronze
The fact that this statue has its eyes engraved on suggests that it is the earliest known Greek bronze. Later bronzes were also cast whole, but, as with marble figures, features such as glass eyes were added.

MARCUS AURELIUS
161–80 A.D.; larger than life-size; bronze
This is the only existing large-scale Roman bronze. Mistaken for the Christian emperor Constantine during the Middle Ages, it survived the mass plundering of "pagan" statues for their metal. Technically complex, equestrian monuments are difficult to cast. Not only do they tend to be large, but all the weight of the horse and rider has to be carried on the horse's spindly legs.

SIX STAGES OF CASTING
This is a modern reconstruction of the various stages of the *indirect* lost-wax process that Giambologna (1529–1608) used to cast his *Mars* (c.1546).

The original model is made of solid wax on a wire support

Runners and risers create channels in the casting mold for the bronze to flow in and air to escape

Runners and risers

1. The first stage of the indirect process distinguishes it from the direct: an original model is made and preserved so that numerous replicas can be cast. The direct process uses a plaster model that is destroyed during casting.

2. From the original model, another hollow wax figure is cast. Above, this hollow figure has been filled with a liquid plaster and grog (p. 62), which has set in the hollow core. Nails have been driven through the wax, and wax rods known as "runners" and "risers" have been fitted.

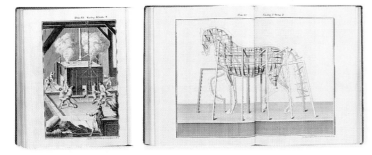 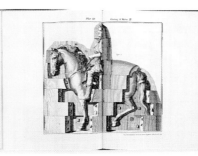 

CASTING ON A LARGE SCALE – THE HORSE

The most effective method of casting a large statue is to build the entire mold into a furnace (see below). The illustrations here are taken from Diderot's encyclopedia. They show the famous equestrian monument of Louis XIV, which was erected in Paris, in 1699.

1. First, a model is built with a complicated internal structure of wrought-iron bands (left) and a plaster cast is constructed around it (above). A wax impression is then taken of the statue in the cast.

2. An external circulatory system of wax runners and vents is attached to the outside surface of the wax shell (see *Mars*, 2, below).

3. This cross-section shows how the bronze replaces the wax in the mold. Covered in heat-resistant plaster and encased in brickwork, the wax is melted out. The runners form a circulatory system, channeling the molten bronze to all areas between the framework and outside plaster mold. The previously hollow shell of wax forms a thin bronze wall.

GATTAMELATA
Donatello; c.1450; 11½ x 13 ft (3.5 x 4 m); bronze
This equestrian monument of a mercenary, known as Gattamelata, was the first to be cast since antiquity. Though it displays a debt to the *Marcus Aurelius*, the horse and rider are individually described. A huge undertaking, Donatello (1386–1466) would have had to send it to a foundry to cast it.

A bronze figure has been cast of the wax figure, including its rods

Bronze can be seen underneath the plaster

The metal runners and risers have to be sawed off

The figure is filed and chased

Finally, the surface is treated with chemicals

The surface of the figure has now changed color

3. The hollow wax figure with the hard core (no. 2) has been baked overnight in a mold; the bronze has been poured in and the wax melted out. Here, the bronze is shown cooling from the furnace, covered in plaster from the casting mold.

4. Now the figure has to be defined: the solid bronze runners and risers have to be sawed off; the nails that hold the core in position must be pulled out, the holes left by them drilled and plugged with bronze; and a larger hole made to remove the hard core from the interior.

5. Though Giambologna employed a bronze founder, Portigiani, to execute the technical aspect of casting, the final finishing would have been done by his studio. There the figure would have been filed and chased (p. 62) to refine its surface and endow it with delicate details.

6. Finally, the whole piece is cleaned with acid – only slightly tarnished, it has the appearance of a newly minted coin. By treating the surface with different chemicals, the artist can change the surface color, prematurely aging the piece. This process is known as "patination."

The medieval figure

AFTER THE FALL OF THE ROMAN EMPIRE, European art was influenced by the Byzantine Empire, in the East (see *Horses of St. Mark's*, p. 25). It was not until medieval times, with power concentrated in the Church and in stable political states that two great styles emerged from Western Europe: the Gothic and the Romanesque. The desire to teach the Bible to the largely illiterate population meant that both styles derived their wealth and inspiration from the Church. Religious pieces adorned the inside and outside of churches (pp. 30–31). Dominated by architecture, Romanesque and early Gothic figure sculpture was stiff and stylized, with little regard for realism or proportion. Sometimes grotesque, it was designed to overwhelm with its spiritual power. With the advent of the Gothic era, however, the Church began to teach that God had made man in His own image and that art should reflect His creation. By the 13th century, this had encouraged the development of a more realistic figure style.

MALE PORTRAIT FROM EPHESUS
c.A.D. 450; 12½ in (31.8 cm); marble
This portrait is typical of the Byzantine period. Stiff and simple in outline, it has large eyes and lightly carved hair. The proportions are governed by strict mathematical guidelines – the body would have been equal to 28 nose lengths. The face is composed of circles, which all have their base on the upper lip and radiate out to describe brow, forehead, hairline, and halo. The Romanesque and Gothic are rooted in the Byzantine stylization of forms, rather than the classical observation of nature (pp. 22–25).

The face is made up of a series of circles

CELTIC CROSS, IRELAND
c.A.D. 750; 12 ft (3.65 m); stone
Beyond the influence of Byzantium, the Celts adapted the symbolic forms of their "native" religion for this cross. The square base denotes the earth, the circles the heaven, and the shaft, the axis of the world.

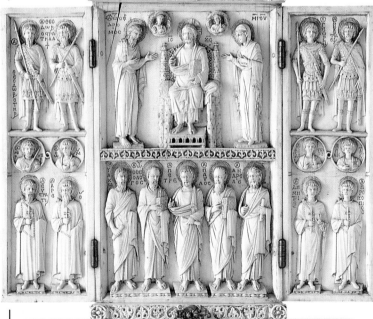

HARBAVILLE TRIPTYCH
c.950; 9½ x 11¼ in (24.2 x 28.5 cm); ivory and gold leaf
This triptych was carved for the emperor in his own workshop in Constantinople. It is centered on the figure of Christ, who is himself represented as a king or emperor, seated on a throne.

PROPHET ISAIAH
c.1130; 69¼ in (176 cm); stone
As the act of worship left the austere monasteries and entered the city cathedrals, so sculptors broke free from some of the more formulaic Romanesque ideals and began to mirror the world around them. A joyful optimism is suggested by this prophet, who dances in an ecstasy reminiscent of the flowing images of ancient Greece.

The soft treatment of the Virgin's face gives her an aristocratic appearance

Christ wears a crown of thorns to emphasize his agony

VESPER IMAGE
c.1300; 10½ in (26.5 cm) high; wood
During the 14th century, death, disease, and famine ravaged Europe. Every household had been touched by the pain of death. Religious sculptures of the time reflect this torment through the exaggerated expressions of the figures. Christ's twisted body, clearly in agony here, is slumped over a distraught Mary.

MADONNA OF KRUMAN
c.1400; 44 in (112 cm) high; stone with traces of polychrome
The end of the 13th century saw the close of a period of great cathedral building, and sculptors turned to the interior to display their works. The break with architecture revived an interest in movement and complicated arrangements of drapery. The figure shape became fuller and softer. Here the S-shape composition creates harmony and balance. The Madonna is transformed into a genteel lady with golden hair, a porcelain complexion, and lightly rouged cheeks.

GROUP ATTENDING CRUCIFIXION
c. 1400; 14 in (36 cm) high; alabaster
This group is thought to have been sculpted by the Italian Master of Rimini, in Germany. At the time it was made, art was undergoing a transition in Italy, as the Renaissance began. Gothic sculpture, however, continued to be produced in Northern Europe into the 15th and 16th centuries. For this reason, some of Italy's more traditional artists traveled north to find work.

Carving the cathedral

THE PROLIFIC PERIOD OF CATHEDRAL building that began in mid-12th-century Europe stimulated an era of intensive sculptural activity. Not only were cathedrals clad or furnished with sculptures, but all their architectural parts were hewn out of stone by stonemasons, presenting infinite opportunities for decorative carving. In France, the construction of taller churches, built with the aid of flying buttresses, created more flexible structures allowing for elaborate stonework. The carvings of Chartres Cathedral, in the Loire region, are so many and so various that they create an entire encyclopedia of sculptural forms. (There are more than 1,800 figure sculptures alone dotted around the building.) After a fire in 1194, most of the church was reconstructed in the 13th-century High Gothic style.

THE WEST ROSE WINDOW
Constructing churches with higher ceilings and flying buttresses made it possible to transform larger expanses of the wall surfaces into windows. Accordingly, the stonework or tracery became more intricate and lacy. In this rose window, which was constructed c.1215, the tracery is still quite prominent from the exterior. The central and larger outer circles form their own roses, and the 12 inner segments are divided by columns.

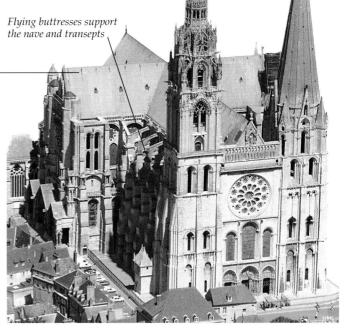

The north steeple

The south steeple

Flying buttresses support the nave and transepts

This transept forms an arm of the cross

LAST SUPPER
Carved into the capital of the right buttress on the west facade's Royal Portal (right), this is one of many scenes that form a frieze across the three doorways. Despite being part of a larger scheme, the *Last Supper* was individually signed "Rogerus." Each figure is framed by the tiny arch above it, and its size relates to its religious importance. Above these arches is a fine cornice of small Gothic leaves, known as crockets.

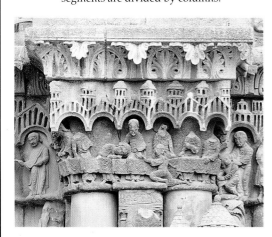

STATUE BASES ON THE NORTH PORCH
Sculpted during the initial stages of building work on the new cathedral (c.1200–25), these statue bases on the jambs of the north porch show a new delight in depicting natural details. By carving deeply, the sculptor was able to render each object intricately, defining every leaf on a tree. This contrasts with the statues above, which are rigid and stylized, adopting a columnlike form. Each base symbolizes the saint that it supports. The burning bush, for instance, represents Mary's virginity.

CHARTRES CATHEDRAL
Taken from the northwest, this aerial view of Chartres looks onto the west facade of the cathedral. The 12th-century Royal Portal (right) and bases of the towers are visible, with the 13th-century rose window above (top left). Although the cathedral was originally intended to have nine steeples, only the two that can be seen here were ever built. The 12th-century south steeple contrasts with the more flamboyant Gothic north steeple. Forming a cross, the nave and transept rise up above the top of the west facade. In the shadow of the north steeple and transepts are the flying buttresses that were so essential to the innovative Gothic method of church construction.

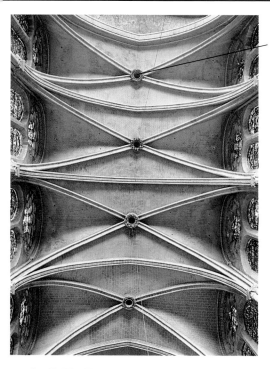

The coping stones are decorated with naturalistic foliage

NAVE CEILING
A greater understanding of the characteristics of stone and increased skill in cutting it allowed for the use of slender supporting ribs. The innovative builders of Chartres broke with tradition and replaced the conventional square bay, divided into six parts, with a rectangle of four sections. This makes the ribs and the lower pillars absorb the total weight of the ceiling, while the exterior buttresses absorb the outward thrust. Using these methods, the height of the ceiling was increased. Although the function of most of these elements was structural, they combined to create an architecture of the utmost elegance, which was centered on the carved and gilded coping stones.

FLYING BUTTRESSES
The most striking external feature of Gothic architecture, the flying buttress, was originally purely decorative. Realizing its architectural potential, the Chartres builders developed the buttress and embellished its surfaces with sculptures and decoration. Here, sentry-box-like recesses, containing ecclesiastical figures, are carved into the buttresses. Higher up, the spokes that attach the flying buttresses to the building are pierced with tracery, making them appear delicately thin and insubstantial.

DEMON AND A LADY OF RANK, DEMON AND NUN
These figures are attached to the inner molding of the central arch in the cathedral's south porch. Built only half a century later than the Royal Portal (below left), the south porch displays dramatic stylistic changes – the figures have lost their vertical emphasis; they move freely, no longer part of the wall. They relate to one another and are better integrated with their surroundings. The theme of the porch is Christ's triumph over evil. Here, grotesque gargoyles and demons are portrayed trying to entice women into wrongdoing. Skillful use of the drill has allowed the sculptor to use the whole block, placing shoulders, hands, and props at the extreme edges. The canopy and pedestal are used to unite the various elements of the scene's composition.

Shadows behind the figures indicate how deeply carved they are

THE ROYAL PORTAL ON THE WEST FACADE
This portal is all that remains of the earlier church. Constructed in the middle of the 12th century, it hints at a transition from the Romanesque to the Gothic. On the whole, its sculpture is far more rigid and ordered than that of the 13th century. The entire design is divided almost equally in half by the horizontal frieze (see *Last Supper*, left). Unlike the figures of the south portal, which appear to be escaping from the architecture (see *Demon and a Lady of Rank*, above right), the sculptures are incorporated into the architectural elements.

ARISTOTLE
This figure of the Greek philosopher Aristotle is one of seven sculptures of scholars that represent their own particular areas of learning. Decorating the inner molding of the arch on the right of the Royal Portal, they surround a semicircular relief of the "all-seeing vision" of the Virgin and Child.

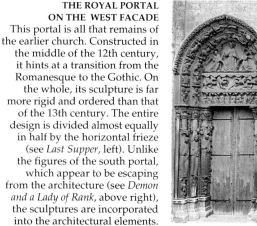

Early Renaissance

THE 15TH CENTURY IN ITALY was a turning point for Western culture. Known as the Early Renaissance, it was a period in which there was a "rebirth" of interest in the art of ancient Rome. Renaissance sculptors captured the spirit of antiquity by reviving the aspirations of the Romans and the Greeks. They did this by producing technically adventurous pieces that depicted their subjects with a new realism. The greatest innovation of the time was perspective, which enabled sculptors to create a convincing illusion of space and depth in a relief (see *Herod's Feast*, top right). Sculptors also revived the difficult technique of casting large-scale figures in bronze (see *David*, near right). One of the richest mercantile cities in northern Italy, Florence was the nucleus of all this artistic activity. The city's civic pride generated a unique climate of public and private patronage, in which competitions were held for important commissions (see below).

THE SACRIFICE OF ISAAC
Lorenzo Ghiberti; 1401; 21¼ x 17½ in (53.5 x 44.5 cm); gilded bronze
This is the winning entry for the competition of 1401 that determined the maker of a pair of doors for the Florence Baptistery. Positioned opposite Florence Cathedral, the doors were a prestigious commission. Although only these two reliefs, by Lorenzo Ghiberti (1378–1455) and Filippo Brunelleschi, (1377–1446), survive seven artists originally competed. The entrants had the difficult task of designing a dramatic Old Testament scene within this awkward quatrefoil-shape frame.

HERCULES AND ANTAEUS
Antonio del Pollaiuolo;
1470s; 18 in (45 cm) high; bronze
This statue, which is an exercise in depicting anatomy in motion, shows how, by the end of the century, sculptors had become interested in studying human form and movement.

THE SACRIFICE OF ISAAC
Filippo Brunelleschi; 1401; 21¼ x 17½ in (53.5 x 44.5 cm); gilded bronze
It was Ghiberti's technical expertise that won him the competition. While Ghiberti was able to cast the relief in one piece, each part of Brunelleschi's scene was made separately and soldered into place. Although Ghiberti's relief is certainly more successful than Brunelleschi's, they both lack unity in their composition, which is characteristic of the Early Renaissance. Ghiberti did make some attempt to counteract this by linking the foreground and background figures with a rock.

FEAST OF HEROD
Donatello; c.1425; 23½ x 23½ in (60 x 60 cm); gilded bronze
Here, Donatello used the subtle gradations of shallow bronze relief and the newly discovered perspective to help tell his story. The architecture creates three moments in time: in the background St. John the Baptist is executed, while musicians play in the middle ground and Herod's feast takes place in the foreground.

THE COLLEONI MONUMENT
Andrea del Verrocchio; c.1481–96; 13 ft (3.95 m); bronze
This statue was made for a prominent square in Venice to commemorate the recent death of Colleoni, a successful mercenary. Though the equestrian monument is a classical sculpture type used to celebrate victorious leaders (pp. 26–27), the details here, such as the armor and breed of horse, were entirely contemporary.

The laurel leaves symbolize the Medici who commissioned the sculpture

MARZOCCO LION
Donatello; 1418–20; 53¼ in (135.5 cm) high; stone
The government of Florence commissioned this heraldic symbol of the city to stand in the Pope's Florentine apartments. With a gilded crown and swirling mane, the lion was an image of stylized magnificence.

With their left hands placed on their hips, both Davids adopt similar poses

DAVID
Donatello; c.1440; 62¼ in (158 cm) high; bronze
Naked except for his hat and his boots, this *David* was probably the first freestanding, fully three-dimensional nude since Roman times. The Old Testament figure of David was a recurring theme for the Florentines, as it had republican connotations. The laurels in his hat and the wreath were symbols of the Medici family, in whose palace the statue was seen in 1469.

The intricate patterns on the tunic display Verrocchio's casting skills

DAVID
Andrea del Verrocchio; c.1470; 49¼ in (125 cm) high; bronze
Also commissioned by the Medici family, this clothed *David* by Andrea del Verrocchio (1435–88) rivaled Donatello's earlier version. Verrocchio's statue lacks the sensuousness of Donatello's, but Verrocchio, who originally trained as a goldsmith, impresses the viewer with his craftsmanship. Perfectly cast, this *David* has an exquisite finish.

Terra-cotta

S INCE THE STONE AGE, sculptors have exploited the sensitivity of terra-cotta clay to heat and water. Malleable and easy to model when wet, clay has only to be fired to become hard and durable. Available worldwide, it has a "commonplace" status. Often used for domestic pots and preparatory sculptural models, it does not have the intrinsic value of bronze or marble. Clay's tendency to shrink and crack means that only smaller works can be made solid. Larger pieces have to be cast hollow in a mold or built on a framework, known as an armature (p. 62). After an initial firing, color can be applied to clay with glaze – a mixture of oxidized tin, lead, sand, and pigment. In Europe, terra-cotta was only elevated to a fine art form during the 15th century, when the Florentine sculptor Luca della Robbia (1400–82) started applying glazes used for pottery to architectural decorations and statues. Non-Western cultures developed their own distinct ceramic traditions (p. 12).

MAJOLICA PLATE
It is no accident that enameled terra-cotta was adopted by sculptors in Florence. The towns of northern Italy were famous for their majolica – finely decorated tin-glazed earthernware. During the 15th century, majolica grew increasingly complex in design and in its range of colors. This brightly colored bowl of 1515 from Deruta (central Italy) depicts a classical scene.

THE LAUGHING CHILD
Antonio Rossellini; c.1465; 19 in (48.5 cm) high; terra-cotta
This was made as a sketch model for a larger sculpture. Clay modeling – an additive process – is flexible and better suited to working out ideas than carving, which is subtractive. The shape of the armature that supports the figure can only be detected from the back, where there is a recess.

The clay falls in intricate folds to suggest drapery

The della Robbia plaques often have blue backgrounds

This is the white underglaze

MADONNA AND CHILD
Andrea della Robbia; 1475; 52½ x 37½ in (134 x 96 cm); enameled terra-cotta
Andrea della Robbia (1435– 1525), as the nephew and pupil of Luca, inherited the della Robbia workshop and continued practicing the technique of making polychrome terra-cottas. (This was done by applying colored glazes to clay sculptures coated in a white base.) Although not as technically proficient as his uncle, Andrea popularized the medium. By molding pieces rather than hand-modeling them, he mass-produced devotional images of the Madonna and Child. In spite of the fact that Andrea's work tended to be less sophisticated and more sentimental than Luca's; he delighted in intricate decoration, such as the garland that frames the Madonna here.

ST. JOHN THE EVANGELIST

Luca della Robbia; 1459–61;
enameled terra-cotta

Light in weight and intensely colored, enameled terra-cotta is perfectly suited to architectural decoration. The colors are not only more brilliant than those of wall paintings, they are also more permanent, as they are fixed in glaze. This roundel is one of four that depict the Evangelists with their symbols. Placed high up in the Pazzi Chapel (below right), just beneath the dome, the Evangelists are larger and more complex than Luca della Robbia's earlier 12 roundels of the apostles for the lower wall. The range of colors is brighter, and the attention to detail greater. The portrayal of the Evangelists is so realistic that it has been suggested that they were in fact modeled by Brunelleschi (p. 32). In any case, there is no doubt that whoever designed the roundels would have had them made up in the della Robbia workshop.

TOOLS

Before firing, wet clay can be easily manipulated. The tools, which have changed little over the centuries, are shaped for specific uses. Wooden tools are used to fold, press, or score the clay, while thick wire is used for cutting.

PIGMENTS

During the 15th century, there was a limited range of glazes available. The colors for glazes were obtained from pigments that had to withstand high temperatures when they were fired. The most successful colors were yellow and blue. They were the most common glazes applied to majolica and terra-cotta.

yellow
pigment

blue
pigment

THE PAZZI CHAPEL

This chapel, which is attached to Santa Croce in Florence, was designed by Brunelleschi in 1433 with circular spaces for roundels. As the only decorative works that Brunelleschi provided for, the terra-cotta reliefs are contrived to punctuate the perfect proportions of the chapel's gray moldings with splashes of color.

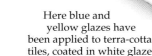

Here blue and yellow glazes have been applied to terra-cotta tiles, coated in white glaze

The High Renaissance

Despite being the most influential period in Western sculpture, the High Renaissance was also one of the shortest. Centered in Rome, it began in about 1500 and ended 27 years later with the sack of the city; its fortunes were closely linked with the capital of the Catholic Church. When Julius II (far right) became Pope in 1503, he was determined to embellish and transform Rome. Though sculpture in 15th-century Florence had been innovative, exploring perspective and the revival of classical forms, the individual parts of a work often appeared unrelated as they lacked an overall unity (see *Sacrifice of Isaac* reliefs, p. 32). High Renaissance sculptors were able to absorb the technical advances of the previous century and execute their works with an ease that resulted in a supreme harmony. The achievements of Michelangelo Buonarroti (1475–1564), a Florentine who was brought to Rome by Julius II, dominate the High Renaissance. His sculpture is remarkable, not only for its balance, but also for its heroic spirit and sense of tension and movement.

RONDANINI PIETA
Michelangelo; 1564; 76¾ in (195 cm) high; marble
Having roughed out a Pietà in the 1550s, Michelangelo abandoned it until a few weeks before his death in 1564. Aged 89 and ill, he changed it radically, replacing its classical grace with insubstantial ethereal bodies and uncomfortable poses.

MICHELANGELO SKETCH
This sketch for another Pietà was drawn in 1552. Before carving directly into stone, Michelangelo tested out his ideas for sculptures with "working drawings" such as this.

PIETA
Michelangelo; 1499;
68½ x 76¾ in (174 x 195 cm); marble
Michelangelo solves the problem of this subject – the Virgin supporting the dead, adult Christ – by using a triangular composition and placing Christ across Mary's lap. His body forms a classical *contrapposto* pose (p. 62): planes contrast, creating emotion and movement. His relaxed position – that of a child asleep – is echoed by arms and drapes. When Michelangelo heard this work had been attributed to another sculptor, he carved across Mary's strap, "Michelangelo Buonarroti, Florentine, made this."

DYING SLAVE
Michelangelo; 1505–13;
90 in (229 cm) high; marble
With sensuous abandon, this slave seems to slip toward death. His final gesture, and the fluency of line from his raised elbow to hip, embody the heroic struggle to live. The head of the ape next to his left knee represents man's animal nature, to which the slave is tied. One of a pair, the slave was commissioned by Pope Julius II for his own tomb. Due to the Pope's early death, other commissions, and the colossal size of the venture (the marble, brought from the quarries at Carrara, filled half of St. Peter's Square), the work was never completed.

THE MEDICI CHAPEL
Michelangelo; 1519–34
Built in Florence as a mausoleum for the Medici family, this chapel is the ultimate realization of High Renaissance harmony. Sculpture and architecture are conceived as one integrated scheme. The interior is treated as a sculptural mass; the elements appear as carved forms rather than structures.

POPE JULIUS
Raphael; 1512; 42½ x 31¼ in
(108 x 81cm); oil on canvas
Despite their regular quarrels – both men had fiery tempers – a strong friendship grew up between Michelangelo and his chief patron, Julius II.

DAVID
Michelangelo; 1504;
161 in (409 cm) high; marble
Made large to exalt man, the power of Michelangelo's *David* lies in its pose – the rhythm of the body, the turn of the wrist, and the quick flash of anger in the frown. Idealized, David is depicted as an athletic youth, rather than as a boy; sling in hand, he is just about to slay Goliath. Originally intended for one of the buttresses of Florence Cathedral, the statue was carved from a single colossal block of marble discarded by the sculptor Agostino di Duccio in 1464.

WAX LEG
Attributed to Michelangelo;
early 16th century; 9½ in
(24 cm) long; wax
As they started to study the proportions of the human figure, Renaissance sculptors began to use wax models and drawings to sketch muscles and poses from life. Here, wires support individually modeled muscles. The leg is of such athletic perfection that it is probably idealized.

Marble

As ONE OF THE MOST ATTRACTIVE and luxurious stones, marble is traditionally used for monumental works. Hard and durable, it can be polished for a highly finished effect. Its crystalline composition means that it can be cut into thin slabs for reliefs, or into large blocks for sculptures. Favored by the Greeks and Romans for architecture, as well as sculpture, marble is often associated with the antique and classical revivals of the Renaissance (pp. 36–37), the Baroque (pp. 42–43), and the Neo-Classical. While it can be mined from the earth's surface with ease, it has one drawback – its weight. At three tons per cubic yard, special methods have had to be contrived to lift marble from the mine.

In the past, the journey from the quarry to the studio was hazardous and expensive, often resulting in breakage. In the 14th century, the transportation costs for marble were as much as the stone itself. However, the tools and techniques used on a block, once it has reached a sculptor's studio, have changed little since the Stone Age (pp. 8–9).

CARRARA
Michelangelo picked his marble from the quarries at Carrara, in Italy. Choosing a block requires experience. The perfect block is of even color, with little or no veining, and no hairline cracks.

APOLLO AND DAPHNE
Gianlorenzo Bernini; 1622–24; 19 ft (2.5 m) high; marble
Despite the detail and smooth surface of this sculpture, Gianlorenzo Bernini (1598–1680) would not have started carving with the chisel and drill – the tools that created these effects. The initial stages of sculpting have always been "roughing out." This is done with a pitching hammer, a point, and then a steel or bronze hammer for areas demanding greater subtlety.

This convex relief takes the form of a bellied Renaissance mirror

DETAIL OF DAPHNE'S HAIR AND FINGERS
Bernini was very proud of the light, delicate effect of Daphne's hair. It was only possible with the use of the drill, which can delicately remove large quantities of marble from areas inaccessible to the chisel, without a jarring movement.

Chisel marks differentiate the rough texture of stone from the smooth surface of skin

THE DRILL BOW
As essential and universal tools, drill bows can be used on all sorts of materials. The Inuit (Eskimo), for instance, used them to make holes in the ice for fishing (p.11).

Michelangelo's original tools

TOOLS
After the initial stages of roughing out, a sculptor sets about defining a sculpture by progressing through a variety of chisels, drills, and rasps. The surface is then given its translucent glow by being polished with pumice stone.

Here, the relief is at its deepest, creating a shadow beneath the Virgin's chin

AWAKENING SLAVE
Michelangelo Buonarroti; 1528; 8¾ ft (2.6 m) high; marble
Michelangelo's working methods are evident in this unfinished work, which was carved at from the front. Michelangelo is supposed to have checked the progress of his statues by sinking their wax preparatory models into vessels of water, and then using the water line to indicate how much of a figure should be freed from the block at a particular stage.

Pitti Tondo

MICHELANGELO *c.1504–05; c.33½ in (85 cm) diameter; marble*

Michelangelo abandoned the drill in 1500, arguing that this tool dominated the sculptor and suffocated the artistic process. Instead, he used a variety of chisels, claiming that God was guiding his hand as he freed the sculptures from the stone. He used the claw chisel in the way that a painter uses pen and ink, crossing over the surface, redefining features – leaving fine parallel grooves (see detail of Christ's leg, below), which could later be smoothed down with rasps (p. 62).

DETAIL OF CHRIST'S HEAD
Because Michelangelo avoided using the drill, he defined hair archaically with a chisel. The angelic features of Christ, however, were carved in such a masterly way that even in their rough state, they needed no embellishment. The young St. John the Baptist appears in low relief, peeping out from behind the Virgin's shoulder, echoing the Christ child.

DETAIL OF CHRIST'S LEG
The use of the claw chisel is clearly visible here in the fine crosshatching of the drapery fold and Christ's lower leg, and the larger grooves that form the background to the tondo. Compared to the ordinary chisel that removes chunks of stone with a single blow, and can easily ride out of control in unskilled hands, the claw chisel chips away small quantities with each knock (p. 62).

These deep folds display Michelangelo's expertise with a chisel

Mannerism

Giambologna displayed his skill with these outstretched arms. Unsupported limbs are difficult to carve in marble as they tend to break off

MANNERISM CANNOT BE DEFINED by its dates alone. Although sculptures do not demonstrate Mannerist ideals before 1520, or after 1600, not every work during this 80-year period could be termed Mannerist. Originating in Italy, Mannerism derived its name from the Italian word *maniera,* meaning style or stylish, and was used by the art biographer Giorgio Vasari (1511–74) to suggest elegance or sophistication. Although Mannerist artists have been condemned by art historians for flouting the High Renaissance ideals of serenity, balance, and calm (p. 36–37), they initially set out to surpass their predecessors' sense of beauty by placing a new emphasis on imagination rather than study from life. The result was a figure sculpture of bizarre poses, overemphasized muscles, and exaggerated proportions. The display of emotion was central, as narrative was overshadowed by dramatic movements and multiple viewpoints.

These tight curls were carved with a drill

RAPE OF THE SABINE WOMEN HEAD (DETAIL)
The abandonment of the Renaissance ideals of tight compositions and simplified features brought about the return of the drill (p. 36). Sculptors could remove stone without a jarring motion and render complicated poses and delicate details – hair, strained muscles, and tortured facial expressions.

RAPE OF THE SABINE WOMEN
Giambologna; before 1583; 162 in (411.5 cm) high; marble
Choosing one of the most difficult poses imaginable, Giambologna (1529–1608) carved this group from a single block of stone. The forms of the figures contrast with one another, twisting and spiraling upward, providing multiple viewpoints; the exaggerated poses cast shadows, highlighting the movement, emotion, and drama.

The twisting figures combine to create a spiraling mass

The rich use of gold epitomizes the opulence of Mannerism

SALT CELLAR
Benvenuto Cellini; c 1540-44; 10¼ x 13¼ in (26 x 33.5 cm); gold, enamel, and ebony
Initially trained as a goldsmith, Benvenuto Cellini (1500–71) worked at the court of Francis I in France. He made many small pieces – coins, medals, and tableware. Here, he combined his sculptural knowledge of the human figure with the intricacies of goldsmithing.

MEDUSA'S HEAD

Here, Medusa is depicted moments after her death – eyes closed and mouth open, viscous entrails dripping from her decapitated head. Only the slithering snakes retain any sign of life. Immensely proud of this fantastic modeling, Cellini had to take great care when casting to ensure that all the detail was retained in the completed bronze. He did this by making more air vents and raising the cast higher in the furnace (pp. 26–27).

Cellini spares us no details – entrails hang from the head

PERSEUS

Benvenuto Cellini; 1545–54; 10½ ft (3.2 m) high; bronze and marble

Perseus's sword breaks up this compact composition and cuts across the contours of the figure. The central placement of the weapon charges the piece with dramatic tension. Perseus himself is shown as an idealized young athlete with a well-defined torso and legs. By contrast, Medusa's body writhes in a contorted position; the arms and legs are only just retained by the plinth. Raised on an elaborate base, *Perseus* was originally intended to be seen from eight different viewpoints.

CELLINI'S AUTOBIOGRAPHY

Cellini wrote treatises on sculpture, design, and the goldsmith's art. But his most celebrated work is his vivid, direct, and often racy autobiography.

Not just limp or stone dead, the body writhes in agony

Blood gushes from the statue

PERSEUS IN SITU

The complicated pose and fantastic detailing of *Perseus* resulted in a long and difficult casting process. Adapting and improving on casting methods learned in France, Cellini built his own molds and furnace, adding more air vents and pouring mouths than was usual (pp. 26–27). But the vast quantity of bronze needed never quite melted. In desperation, Cellini flung in all his household pewter to reduce the melting point. Despite Cellini's pessimistic forecasts, the sculpture emerged perfect in every detail – except for an incomplete right foot! It finally won a prominent position in the Loggia dei Lanzi, in Florence, between Michelangelo's *David* and Donatello's *Judith and Holofernes*.

Power and the Church

THE 17TH CENTURY witnessed the emergence of a new style – the Baroque. Originating in Rome, it grew out of the renewed confidence of the Catholic Church after the trauma of the Reformation. With its religious subjects, dynamic movement, and theatrical effects, it was designed to inspire and impress growing congregations. Large-scale designs were at their most imposing when they combined sculpture with architecture and painting to create a grand unity (see Cornaro Chapel, left). As the style matured, it was applied to increasingly secular subjects. The international influence of Catholicism led to the spread of the Baroque throughout Italy and Europe, and even beyond to the American colonies (pp. 44–45). Outside Rome, it was adopted by kings who realized its potential to affirm regal power. Nowhere was the Baroque more grandiose than in the palace and gardens of Versailles (right), built outside Paris by Louis XIV of France.

THE CORNARO CHAPEL
When Gianlorenzo Bernini (1589–1680) was commissioned to design this chapel, dedicated to St. Teresa of Avila, in Sta Maria della Vittoria, Rome, he was given a unique opportunity to create his own setting for his sculpture. Despite the fact that the interior is overwhelmingly rich in its use of colored marble inlays, architectural features, and gilt, all the elements are devised to frame and draw the eye to *St. Teresa* (right).

Here, the angel retrieves his arrow from St. Teresa, who is at the height of her ecstasy

THE ECSTASY OF ST. TERESA
Gianlorenzo Bernini; 1645–52; 11½ ft (3.5 m) high; marble
In this work Bernini used every available device to spiritually enlighten and impress the viewer. The white marble sculpture and surrounding golden rays are illuminated from above by a concealed window so that the scene appears as a mystic, glowing vision in the dark interior of the chapel (see above). This amount of direct control over the light source is unusual for a sculpture, and it enhances the work with the type of dramatic light effects that can generally only be found in oil paintings of the period. By emphasizing St. Teresa's physical responses to her spiritual experience, Bernini isolated a single moment of climax and drama for the viewer. St. Teresa is shown responding to the angel's arrow with complete bodily abandon; collapsing in an attitude of sensuous passion, she has her head thrown back, her mouth open, and eyes closed. All the surfaces are refined so that the textures of the flesh, cloth, and rock are distinguishable.

The decorative magnificence of the dragon belies the fact that it is writhing in pain

ATLANTEAN FIGURES
Lucas von Hildenbrandt; 1714–21; marble
These Herculean figures in the Belvedere Palace, Vienna, are very different from the serene caryatids of ancient Greece (p. 23). Deeply carved and modeled, they have highly defined muscles, which combine with the elaborate drapes to create dramatic light effects. True to the Baroque style, the figures are charged with theatrical emotion: their exaggerated poses emphasize the colossal weight that they carry.

THE DRAGON FOUNTAIN
Gaspar and Balthazar Marsy; 1666–68; lead
The fountains at Versailles dramatize complex allegories associated with Apollo, who, as "nature's sovereign," was the role model of Louis XIV. This clawed monster is the only original sculpture in an elaborate group of figures that was positioned around a circular pool (below). Even though the dragon is separated from the cherub archers that are attacking it, it writhes in a convincing agony with its head thrown back and tail curled.

Veüe et perspective des Cascades et du Bassin du Dragon a Versailles

The Elector's curls are swept back from his face by the movement of the horse

THE DRAGON FOUNTAIN AND VERSAILLES
When Louis XIV built the palace of Versailles (1669–85), he enlisted André Le Notre (1613–1700) to create a garden that would reflect the symmetry of the architecture. Sculpture anchored the layout, leading the eye from one pathway to the next by punctuating it with fountains and statuary.

THE GREAT ELECTOR
Andreas Schlüter; 1698–1709; bronze
The ability of monumental works to express power, majesty, and permanence brought them back into favor during the Baroque era. Set within architectural surroundings, the monument could become an important focal point, promoting the power of political leaders in towns and cities. This equestrian statue was erected to commemorate Frederick William I of Prussia. Although it is now positioned in a courtyard of Charlottenberg, in Berlin, it originally stood on a bridge over the Spree River near the royal palace. Placed high on a plinth in this public place, the sculpture forced the viewer to look up and confront an image of supreme monarchy – forging ahead, looking through and past his subjects.

Public grandeur

ST. PETER'S PIAZZA, ROME
Bernini (p. 42) used stately classical columns to create the curving colonnades, which define the space in front of the Basilica of St. Peter's. This awe-inspiring piazza is large enough to hold ceremonial processions and vast numbers of pilgrims.

AIR VIEW OF THE PIAZZA NAVONA, ROME
Nine narrow streets empty into this elongated horseshoe-shaped piazza, which was built on the site of an ancient Roman stadium. Though the buildings that surround it are all of differing proportions, a sense of balance and unity is created by the three central fountains.

DURING THE 17TH CENTURY, sculpture took on a greater importance in the urban landscape. While fountains and decorated facades had previously existed as separate features in towns, they now began to be conceived as part of a greater architectural vision, which made individual buildings into unified streets and squares. Placed at the end of vistas or in the center of piazzas, sculptural monuments provided vital focal points. In Rome, there was a particularly pressing cosmetic and practical demand for broad thoroughfares and magnificent squares. The narrow streets and overhanging houses of the old medieval town were inadequate and inappropriate for the capital of the Catholic Church. It was the provision of a new water supply that enabled Rome to be transformed into a city of fountains. Europe's rulers followed suit and began enriching the center of their capitals. In the colonies, towns were built from scratch in a style that impressed native populations with their grandeur and "civilized" symmetry.

This is the base of an antique obelisk

The rivers adopt contrasting poses

PIAZZA NAVONA
The *Four Rivers Fountain* was not the first monument to be constructed in the Piazza Navona; Giacomo della Porta (c.1537–1602) had built the *Fountain of the Moor* in 1575. It was Pope Innocent X (1644–55), however, who deliberately set out to aggrandize and transform the public space with fountains of such magnificence that they became the piazza's main attraction.

FOUR RIVERS FOUNTAIN
Gianlorenzo Bernini; 1648–51; travertine and marble
Bernini's fountain acts as a base for an antique obelisk that Innocent X had moved from another piazza in Rome. In its new context, the stone needle is transformed into a Christian symbol of divine light. The dove that crowns it is Innocent X's emblem, but also represents the Holy Spirit. Below, four massive figures personify the four great rivers of the world. This fountain is such an extravaganza of sculpture and water that during the 18th century the piazza became the site of an annual water festival.

THE PLAGUE COLUMN
Mathias Rauchmiller; 1693
Although this monument does not spout water, it fulfills a function similar to the *Four Rivers Fountain*. Freestanding, it is positioned in the Graben, the old food market of Vienna, where it provides the main focus for the public space. Its vertical structure and the hectic movement of the figures attract the eye upward to the Holy Trinity at the top of the column. First erected by Emperor Leopold I, it commemorates the Great Plague of 1679.

Scrolls decorate the sides of the column's base

THE SEMINARY COLLEGE OF SAN TELMO, SEVILLE
In Spain, the church took the most prominent position in a town's main square. Most sculptural decoration was concentrated on the exterior of the church and its associated buildings. The richly carved portal on this facade displays the Spanish love of dense patterning. Built between 1724 and 1734 by Leonardo de Figueroa, the seminary had a strong influence on Spanish-American architecture. During the 18th century, Seville was the administrative capital of Spain's overseas territories.

The top of the facade is cut out against the sky

Figures are positioned in front of the architectural elements

MEXICO CATHEDRAL, DETAIL
Built between 1572 and 1813 on the site of an Aztec sun temple, Mexico Cathedral was designed by a succession of Spanish architects. With its many facades, such as the one above, it formed a solid block of ornamentation, which grew up organically, rather than following a rigid overall plan.

MEXICO CATHEDRAL
In Mexico, vast tracts of land were available for towns. Built in a checkerboard design, often on the site of Aztec cities, the streets intersected at right angles. There was, however, little sense of progression from one space to another. The central square of Mexico City, for instance, shown here, had no radiating streets. It relied on the the decorative exteriors of the cathedral and the neighboring buildings for its magnificence.

A new classicism

THE NEO-CLASSICAL MOVEMENT was initiated in Rome by intellectuals. Its main propagandist was a German historian, Johann Winckelmann (1717–68), who called on artists to re-create the genius of the ancient Greeks. His belief in the superiority of classical cultures dominated the Neo-Classical period and distinguished it from the earlier Renaissance and Baroque antique revivals (pp. 32 & 42). In sculpture, Neo-Classicism placed a new emphasis on restraint and precision. However, it was the discovery of the archaeological sites at Pompeii, Herculaneum, and Paestum in southern Italy (1738–56) that fueled the fashion for all things classical. Throughout Europe, the wealthy displayed their taste and education by acquiring antique-style objects.

DENIS DIDEROT
Jean-Antoine Houdon; 1771;
16 in (41 cm) high; marble
The French sculptor Jean-Antoine Houdon (1741–1828) was the most highly esteemed portraitist of his time. Here, he used the classical portrait bust to bestow an antique dignity on this very individual depiction of a man.

POMPEII
The ruins of this ancient city became an important stop on the Grand Tour for visitors from as far away as England. Artists, architects, and even furniture makers drew inspiration from the interiors and streets that were recovered.

MONUMENT TO THE PRINCESSES OF MECKLENBURG-SCHERWIN
Gottfried Schadow; 1795; 5½ ft (1.7 m) high; marble
The Prussian royal family commissioned Gottfried Schadow (1764–1850), who was famous for his overt sentimentalization of classical beauty, to make this portrait of the two princesses. Dressed in identical antique-style robes, the two girls are distinguished by their poses. The upright stance of Louise is contrasted with the coy, downward glance of Frederike.

MENACING CUPID
Etienne-Maurice Falconet;
1757; 36 in (91.5 cm) high; marble
This playful, chubby cherub was made by Etienne Falconet (1716–1791) for Madame de Pompadour, the official mistress of the French king Louis XV. Between 1757 and 1766, Falconet transferred this image of the *Menacing Cupid* into a more decorative form by making a whole series of cherubs in biscuit porcelain when he worked as chief modeler for the royal porcelain factory. Most of the porcelain statuettes were made as table ornaments.

These dots are point marks, made by a pointing machine

CLASSICAL COLLECTORS

The discovery of the ruins in Pompeii and Rome led to the widespread pillaging of any salable classical items. These filtered into the collections of some of the wealthiest men in Europe. Charles Towneley, painted by Zoffany, here with his friends at his home in Park Street, London, bought most of his antiquities during the dispersal of the spoils of Hadrian's Villa, in Rome. To acquire these original sculptures, his purse had to compete with royalty and the Pope.

THE THREE GRACES

Antonio Canova; 1813;
5¼ ft (1.65 m) high; plaster
The classical revival coincided with the introduction of precise measuring methods. Assistants made this plaster statue from a full-size maquette by Antonio Canova (1757–1822) and then used it to translate their master's design into marble with the aid of the newly developed open-cage pointing machine (see method of copying a model into marble, below).

ANATOMICAL SKETCH

This sketch is taken from an Italian pattern book that provided sculptors with diagrams for modeling figures with perfectly proportioned bodies.

METHOD OF COPYING A MODEL INTO MARBLE

This is an illustration from an Italian handbook for sculptors, showing how a statue can be transformed from its clay model into marble with the aid of plumb lines and different-sized calipers (p. 62). This particular method was outmoded by the open-cage pointing machine, which encased a marble block and maquette in separate wooden cages. A movable pointer was suspended from the central vertical of both cages so that specific points could be correlated.

MONUMENT TO VISCOUNTESS FITZHARRIS

John Flaxman;
1816–17; life-size; marble
Though John Flaxman (1755–1826) was English, his work was informed by a first-hand knowledge of classical antiquity. He had not only traveled to Rome, but lived there for seven years. At first glance this piece does not appear classical. This is because the Viscountess is presented as a paragon of contemporary familial virtue; caring and cultured, she reads to her older children, while holding a younger child. However, the choice of material – a pure white marble – is true to ancient Greek sculpture, and the Viscountess' curls and empire-line dress evoke antique fashions.

The monumental

ALTHOUGH THE ROMANS realized the propaganda value of nationalistic monuments (pp. 24–25), sculptural elements and styles were not consciously manipulated to reflect the aspirations of society until the 19th century. Classicism was then favored for works that evoked the glory of imperial or republican power (see *Arch of Triumph*, right). The large scale of these sculptures meant that they were often better known as engineering feats than as art. In the 20th century, monuments have represented entire ideologies, such as Communism, but have also become important as tourist attractions.

THE ARCH OF TRIUMPH
François Rude; 1806–36;
164 x 147½ ft (50 x 45 m); stone
Originally designed for Napoleon I, this arch was built in the center of Paris as a testament to the greatness of the French empire. It was made twice as large as the Roman Arch of Constantine (A.D. 315), from which it took its form.

The drapery is made
from stiff sheets
of copper

STATUE OF LIBERTY
Frederic Bartholdi; 1886; 305 ft (93 m)
high; copper sheets and metal frame
Presented to the American people by the French, this statue is the ultimate symbol of republican democracy. Holding a torch, Liberty is personified as a woman in classical robes. She was constructed on a frame built by Gustave Eiffel (1832–1923), the engineer of the Eiffel Tower.

The use of aluminum,
a light metal, makes
it possible to balance
the figure on one foot

Eros's semi-nudity
initailly caused a
public scandal

EROS
Alfred Gilbert; 1886–93; 6.1 ft (1.9 m)
high; aluminum and bronze
This statue does not commemorate a war hero or national event, but a British politician and social reformer – Lord Shaftesbury. Alfred Gilbert (1854–1934) chose the symbol of love to illustrate and emphasize the Earl's compassion. Although made out of aluminum, the figure was cast using the traditional lost-wax process (pp. 26–27). Positioned today in Piccadilly Circus, *Eros* has become synonymous with London's West End.

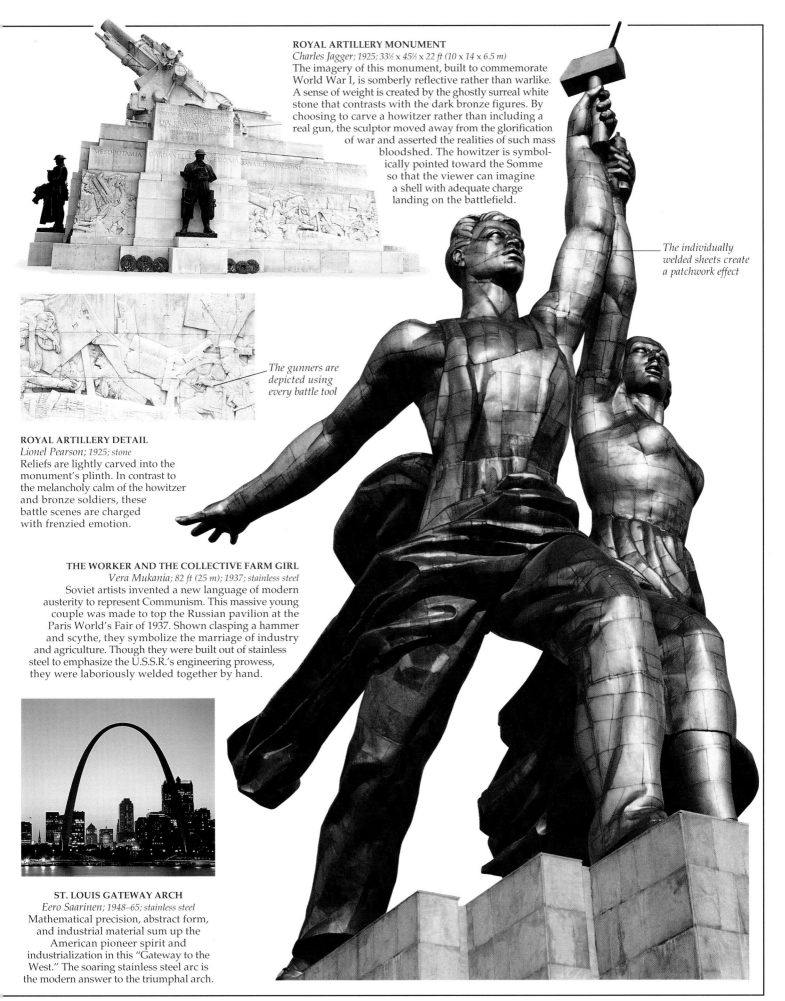

ROYAL ARTILLERY MONUMENT

Charles Jagger; 1925; 33½ x 45½ x 22 ft (10 x 14 x 6.5 m)
The imagery of this monument, built to commemorate
World War I, is somberly reflective rather than warlike.
A sense of weight is created by the ghostly surreal white
stone that contrasts with the dark bronze figures. By
choosing to carve a howitzer rather than including a
real gun, the sculptor moved away from the glorification
of war and asserted the realities of such mass
bloodshed. The howitzer is symbol-
ically pointed toward the Somme
so that the viewer can imagine
a shell with adequate charge
landing on the battlefield.

*The individually
welded sheets create
a patchwork effect*

*The gunners are
depicted using
every battle tool*

ROYAL ARTILLERY DETAIL

Lionel Pearson; 1925; stone
Reliefs are lightly carved into the
monument's plinth. In contrast to
the melancholy calm of the howitzer
and bronze soldiers, these
battle scenes are charged
with frenzied emotion.

THE WORKER AND THE COLLECTIVE FARM GIRL

Vera Mukania; 82 ft (25 m); 1937; stainless steel
Soviet artists invented a new language of modern
austerity to represent Communism. This massive young
couple was made to top the Russian pavilion at the
Paris World's Fair of 1937. Shown clasping a hammer
and scythe, they symbolize the marriage of industry
and agriculture. Though they were built out of stainless
steel to emphasize the U.S.S.R.'s engineering prowess,
they were laboriously welded together by hand.

ST. LOUIS GATEWAY ARCH

Eero Saarinen; 1948–65; stainless steel
Mathematical precision, abstract form,
and industrial material sum up the
American pioneer spirit and
industrialization in this "Gateway to the
West." The soaring stainless steel arc is
the modern answer to the triumphal arch.

New French sculpture

SCULPTORS WERE SLOW to experiment during the 19th century. Not until the very end of the century did they begin to make the dramatic departures that Impressionist painters had made as early as the 1870s. For many years they were hindered by the conservative French academy of art, the Salon, and by their own reliance on public commissions, which often required use of the classical style. Although sculptors could not share the Impressionists' interest in color, they started to reject the study of the classical in favor of exploring surface texture, expression, and light. Among the artists who made this break were the celebrated sculptor Auguste Rodin (1840–1914) and the sculptor and painter Edgar Degas (1834–1917).

THE SALON
Here, Rodin's *Balzac* (far right) can be seen on display in the Louvre, at the Salon of 1898. As the only annual exhibition, the Salon was a society event – people came to look at one other as much as to see works of art.

The twist of the woman's back as she reaches for her lover adds intensity to the embrace

In contrast to the smooth skin, the base is roughly chiseled to look like rock

THE KISS
Auguste Rodin; 1901–4; 5¾ x 3¾ x 4¾ ft (1.8 x 1.2 x 1.5 m); marble
This couple displays such overt passion that the viewer fears disturbing them. The man, strong and muscular, supports and protects the woman; his strength contrasts with a gentle caress, as he touches her thigh. The light, tender kiss counters the woman's passionate embrace. Entwined, the lovers are indistinguishable – as if they were one. Here, Rodin is interested in the expressive power of the whole, rather than showing fine detail. The rock ties the two figures together, giving the piece permanence and solidity.

THE CROUCHING WOMAN
Auguste Rodin; 1892; 21 x 38 x 21 in (53 x 96.5 x 53 cm); bronze
Much of Rodin's work was made up of studies or "fragments." Rodin employed models to relax and stroll around his studio, in the nude, so that he could watch their movements constantly. In fragments such as this he neglected any superfluous details and isolated the areas that particularly interested him.

Rather than being portrayed as a distinguished figure, Balzac has disorderly hair and dreamy eyes

Here, Rodin concentrates on the figure's stretching movement

THE AGE OF BRONZE
Auguste Rodin; 1878; 72¾ x 29 x 20¾ in (185 x 74 x 53 cm); bronze
In this, his first major work, Rodin challenged the Salon on its own grounds. He complied with convention by making it highly finished and anatomically correct, but surpassed classical tradition with the realism of his pose. Observed from a life model, it appears like a single frame that has been isolated from a stream of action shots. When the sculpture was exhibited, he was accused of using a life cast. He denied this – citing his Renaissance studies as the reason for its perfection – but was expelled from the reactionary Salon.

RODIN IN A BALZAC-LIKE COAT
In this photo, Rodin appears three years before his death in 1917. Now world-famous, he had a huge workshop that executed large works, such as *The Kiss*, to his own models.

LITTLE DANCER AGED 14
Edgar Degas; 1880; 39 in (99 cm) high; bronze
Degas' work was cast in bronze only after his death. All his original sculptures were made out of wax and a kind of plasticine, a mixture of clay and oil. By freely mixing in objects from the real world – slippers, tutu – Degas combines traditional sculpture with collage, forcing us to relate to the girl and to become personally involved with the piece.

One of several studies, it shows a dancer examining the sole of her foot

DANCER
Edgar Degas; 1896–1911; bronze
This is a small three-dimensional sketch, which was never meant to gain the status of a work of art. Degas, like Rodin in his "fragments" (top right), was attempting to capture a fleeting moment.

BALZAC
Auguste Rodin; 1897; 8¾ x 3¾ x 4¾ ft (2.7 x 1.2 x 1.3 m); bronze
In 1891, a French literary society awarded Rodin a prestigious commission to sculpt the great novelist Balzac. As Balzac had been dead since 1850, Rodin could not model him from life. However, before deciding to show him cloaked, Rodin made numerous studies. The cloak lends the statue a monumentality and creates dramatic light effects in its folds. Balzac has unruly hair and a vigorous expression, which present him as a Romantic artist rather than a dignified writer. It was this radical portrayal that made the literary society reject the sculpture.

Emergence of the modern

THOUGH SCULPTURE CANNOT BE divorced from the surrounding world, few periods in art have reflected their age as closely as that of the first two decades of the 20th century. A mounting sense of change accompanied the new century and inspired artists to break with existing styles and ideas, in pursuit of the "modern." Sculptors built on Rodin's revolt against the academic and the classical (pp. 50–51) and concerned themselves instead with developing fresh approaches to construction and subject matter. By exhibiting an ordinary urinal, *The Fountain* (top right), in New York, Marcel Duchamp (1887–1968) created the period's greatest artistic controversy. It was Europe, however, that was the true center of intellectual debate and manifesto-making. Paris was its art capital, where artists were constantly experimenting, inventing, and forming themselves into new groups associated with particular styles, such as the Cubists, Constructivists, and Surrealists.

PARISIAN CAFE LIFE
Cafés are the perfect meeting places for artists and writers. With its many cafés and clubs, Paris was an artistic and intellectual mecca. Such was the draw of the city for budding artists that the young Constantin Brancusi spent two years walking there from his home in Romania.

THE KISS
Constantin Brancusi; 1925–34;
14 x 10 x 9½ in (36.5 x 25.5 x 24 cm); stone
This work reacts against Rodin's *Kiss* (p. 50) and the trend for imitating nature. By carving it from a single block, Constantin Brancusi (1876–1957) captures the simplicity of his native folk art and the vitality of non-Western art. The contemporary interest in abstraction at this time led artists to appreciate the simpler forms of "primitive" sculpture.

The visor gives the figure an ominous air, concealing its features

A fetus lies in the hollow of the Rock Drill's open stomach

ROCK DRILL
Jacob Epstein; 1913–14; 28 x 23 x 17½ in
(70.5 x 58.5 x 44.5 cm); torso in metal and bronze
The original version of this work by Jacob Epstein (1880–1957) embodied the ideals of a short-lived art movement known as Vorticism. Based in Britain in the years preceding World War I, the Vorticist group sought inspiration from the machine. Through his "automan," Epstein tried to create a geometric structure expressing speed, activity, and energy through forms made of pistons, levers, grills, and industrial girders. Initially built as a full-length figure, this piece incorporated a real rock drill as an ideal of aggressive, mechanistic power. However, the horrors of World War I made Epstein realize the machine's part in man's destruction, and he dismantled the drill, casting only the torso. By using the top half of the *Rock Drill*, the fetus – Epstein's warning to humanity – was fully exposed, lying unprotected and vulnerable in the stomach.

GUITAR

Pablo Picasso; 1912; 29½ in (75 cm) high; paper, glue, string, and crayon
Cubism was founded in 1907 by Picasso and the French painter Georges Braque (1882–1963). One of the most important modern movements, it broke away from the idea of art imitating nature. It aimed to depict objects as they were known, from many different angles, rather than as they appeared. Although Cubism is less pronounced in sculpture than painting, this piece explores the various planes of a guitar.

The planes of the guitar are at different angles

THE FOUNTAIN

Marcel Duchamp; 1917; porcelain
Duchamp's only intervention was to "sign" this urinal R. Mutt – after an American toilet engineer. By placing an ordinary object – a "ready-made" – on display to be considered in traditional artistic terms, Duchamp promoted the notion that sculpture is reliant on intellect rather than technical, manual skills.

The head resembles an architectural blueprint or technical model

HEAD NO. 2

Naum Gabo; 1916;
5¾ x 4½ x 4 ft (1.75 x 1.35 x 1.23 m); cor-ten steel
In this sculpture, Naum Gabo (1890–1977) embraced the ideas of Constructivism – a Russian movement. By using welded industrial sheets of steel, he described depth, movement, and shade in geometric terms. This technological solution to constructing a head transformed the sculptor into an engineer.

Placed on the handset, this lobster is a visual surprise, appearing totally misplaced

LOBSTER TELEPHONE

Salvador Dali; 1936; 7 x 13 in (17.8 x 33 cm)
Surrealists, such as Salvador Dali (1904–89), used dreams as a source for fantastic and irrational images. Placing unassociated found objects side by side, the artist hoped to shock and excite the viewer.

Postwar Europe

ALTHOUGH ART HISTORIANS today are eager to categorize postwar art into movements, artists of the time were fiercely individual. The development of communications and air travel allowed them to share points of interest while developing into worldly freethinkers. Humbled by the experience of World War II, they turned away from monumental structures and subjects. Preferring to experiment with traditional materials, they looked to ancient and ethnic art to enliven their work with an essential vitality. Some, including Constantin Brancusi (1876–1957), Henry Moore (1898–1986), and Barbara Hepworth (1903–75), allowed the natural properties of a material to dictate the final form. Others, like Alberto Giacometti (1901–66), Eduardo Paolozzi (b. 1924), and Marino Marini (1901–66), became concerned with exploring the more illusive realms of the subconscious.

BARBARA HEPWORTH IN HER STUDIO AT ST. IVES
By unifying natural and abstract forms, Hepworth and Moore attracted the attention of many leading artists in Britain. Highly influential, they soon became known internationally as the St. Ives group, after Hepworth's hometown in Cornwall.

MOTHER AND CHILD
Henry Moore; 1932; 36 in (91.5 cm) high; green hornstone marble
Strongly influenced by non-Western art, Moore stripped his figures down to the minimum – basic, organic shapes of ovals and rounded lines. Expanding on his prewar work, Moore continued to explore the endless theme of the human body and family unit. It led him to develop a style that was quite independent from those of his contemporaries.

OVAL SCULPTURE, NUMBER TWO
Barbara Hepworth; 1943; 11¼ x 16¼ x 10 in (28.5 x 41.5 x 25.5 cm); plaster
Hepworth found constant inspiration in the rugged landscape of the Cornish coastline. Here, sweeping curves and sharp lines direct our eye over the whole form. Like a tide-worn stone on the beach, the surface is pierced – making us aware of the three-dimensional quality of the piece.

THE BIRD
Constantin Brancusi; 1940; 75½ x 5¼ in (191.5 x 13.5 cm); metal
Combining stonelike forms with upward movement and a highly polished surface – reminders of mechanization and new materials – Brancusi jostles the symbols of nature and industry. He perfectly fuses the concept of "modern" flight and the vital form of the bird.

MAQUETTE
Moore made up small models, known as maquettes, to show his ideas for sculptures to clients. This one was made in 1943 for a Madonna and Child.

The pierced objects and the
bow are all cast in bronze –
a traditional material

The naked, simple shape of this
horseman contrasts with the
victorious generals of classical
equestrian monuments (p. 27)

HORSEMAN
*Marino Marini; 1947;
64½ x 61 x 26½ in
(164 x 155 x 67.5 cm); bronze*
This sculpture recalls
Marini's wartime
memories of Italian
peasants watching
Allied planes flying
over their fields. Despite
the modern narrative,
the horseman's
simplified forms have
a timeless, primitive
quality, evocative of
Etruscan (pre-Roman)
art. It is probable that
Marini was trying to
make a link between
contemporary and
ancient experiences.

FORMS ON A BOW
*Eduardo Paolozzi; 1949;
19 x 25 x 8½ in
(48.5 x 63.5 x 21.5 cm); bronze*
Paolozzi, a British sculptor of
Italian parentage, sought relief
from the privations of postwar
Britain by seeking inspiration
abroad. He worked in a variety
of styles, combining the figurative,
abstract, and classical. The bow, which
skewers industrial shapes, marries
together an ancient, fundamental
form with contemporary debris.

WOMAN
*Alberto Giacometti; 1958;
4¼ ft (1.3 m) high; bronze*
Depicted without volume,
Giacometti's figures soar
upward. Emaciated and
isolated, they evoke images
of concentration camp
victims. Giacometti himself
regarded his sculptures as
explorations in light and
shade, created through
the layering and
stripping down of
plaster of Paris strips.
The figures' rough
surfaces gives them
an undetermined,
mysterious quality.

STANDING FIGURE
Giacometti was
influenced by Etruscan
and Iberian (early
Italian and Spanish)
tomb sculptures. His
female figures appear
upright and rigid like
idols, while his male
figures are more active,
walking or pointing.
This drawing, made in
1956, emphasizes the
frame on which the
plaster is modeled.

*Giacometti anchored
his emaciated figures
with solid plinths*

Sculpture in the U.S.A.

In 1913 THE ARMORY SHOW toured the United States, enabling people to see modern European art for the first time in their own country. A remarkable exhibition, it convinced many American artists to travel to Europe. After a period abroad, these artists brought home new ideas that were developed in conjunction with established art traditions. It was not, however, until the Great Depression of the 1930s and World War II that the United States became politically and economically more isolated, and culturally independent. By the 1960s, New York had replaced Paris as the center of the art world. Using materials endowed by a space-age society, different movements grew up, feeding off and reacting to one another. The most important of these were Pop art, which took its inspiration from popular culture, and Minimalism, which set out to question the preconceptions of viewers through the most basic of forms.

The surface is polished to give it a metallic sheen

CUBI XIX
David Smith; 1964;
9½ x 4¼ x 3¼ ft (2.9 x 1.5 x 1 m); metal
As a follower of Abstract Expressionism (p. 62) – a self-consciously American modern art movement – David Smith (1906–65) used basic forms to question the preconceptions and prejudices of the viewer. By making this piece out of industrial steel, Smith avoided any references to traditional European art.

ANTENNAE WITH RED AND BLUE DOTS
Alexander Calder; 1960; 3½ x 4¼ x 4¼ ft (1.1 x 1.3 x 1.3 m); metal
Alexander Calder (1898–1976) was a constant visitor to Paris, where he became influenced by European abstract movements. Originally trained as an engineer, he made his first moving sculpture in 1931, which was dubbed by Marcel Duchamp a "mobile." The plate steel counterweights were designed to move constantly with air currents, providing ever-changing forms.

ANDY WARHOL AND THE FACTORY
During the 1960s, Andy Warhol (1926–1987) was the most influential figure on the American art scene. Regarding himself as a kind of manager, he surrounded himself with helpers in his downtown New York studio, known as the Factory (left). Experimenting with a variety of art forms, from music to film, Warhol directed the manufacturing of Pop art, which used American popular culture as its subject matter.

RUNNING ARCS FOR JOHN CAGE

Richard Serra; 1992; 145½ x 51 x 2 in (370 x 130 x 5.5 cm); steel
As one of the most provocative Minimalist sculptors, Richard Serra (b. 1939) is always intent on grabbing his viewer's attention. His works are positioned by weight and gravity alone, and appear precariously balanced. Here, for instance, the arcs tilt dramatically. These graceful curves, which seem to float across the gallery floor, contrast with the material from which they are made. Constructed from massive rolled plates of steel, the rusted metal bears an industrial manufacturer's mark. By keeping this mark, Serra has emphasized the origin of his chosen material and endowed the pieces with a previous history and personality.

Minimal, this sculpture is no more than a diagonal line

The colored plates are counterbalanced on wire stems so that they move freely in the slightest breeze

The cube's glowing interior is the only feature that invites the viewer's curiosity

BI CD IN CONTRAIL

Carl André; 1991; 4 x 212½ x ½ in (10 x 540 x 1 cm); bismuth, indium, and cadmium
By dividing the floor of the gallery with this diagonal and creating two new "spaces," Carl André (b.1935) asks the viewer to consider the characteristics of the room as well as the form. Like many of André's pieces, this work is made of industrial metals and is arranged on the floor. The public is invited to walk on the sculpture, which allows them an unusual amount of contact with an art object.

UNTITLED

Donald Judd; 1973; 14½ x 76½ x 29½ in (37 x 194.5 x 75 cm); metal
By using a common cube, industrial metals, and modern manufacturing techniques, David Judd (b. 1928) exemplifies Minimalist ideals in this work. The use of precise fixing techniques and ordinary materials makes the idea behind the object, rather than the form itself, most important. If Judd had not placed a colored piece of metal inside this cube – causing the enclosed space to glow – the viewer would barely give the work a second glance. Warm and enticing, the interior invites a closer look. By consistently using these devices, Judd tries to make viewers reexamine their own relationship with form, material, and inner space.

New materials

In the past two decades, sculptors have liberated themselves from using traditional materials such as bronze, wood, and stone. They have purposely set out to investigate the characteristics of new media and techniques. By moving away from casting and carving, they have started to experiment with synthetic and industrial fibers, and metals, which reflect contemporary urban society. These everyday materials have the added advantages of being instantly recognizable and readily available. A full exploration of the nature, color, and form of common materials enables artists to challenge people's preconceived notions about society at large (see *Car Door, Ironing Board and Twin-Tub with North American Indian Head-Dress*, far right). Modern techniques have freed sculptors from concentrating their energies on technical skills, allowing them to focus more intently on the artistic thought processes.

PUPPY
Jeff Koons; 1992; 40 x 16¼ x 21¼ ft (12 x 50 x 65 m); flowers
This 40-foot puppy, constructed out of 17,000 fresh flowers, has none of the usual characteristics of a monumental work. Traditionally, monumental sculpture has a heroic subject and is made out of permanent materials, such as marble or bronze (see pp. 48–49). Jeff Koons heightened the kitschy effect of his *Puppy* by situating it in a grand historic setting, outside Arolsen Castle, in Germany.

Nauman alternates words with opposing meanings

The barred entrance is lit to draw the viewer's attention to it

DO WE TURN ROUND INSIDE HOUSES, OR IS IT HOUSES WHICH TURN AROUND US?
Mario Merz; 1977–85; 8½ x 41¼ ft (2.6 x 5 m); metal, glass, electric light, and stone
Here, Mario Merz (b.1925) presents the glass igloo as a universal symbol of shelter. (Igloo-shaped dwellings are found throughout the world, even in Merz's native Italy, where there are domed stone houses in the Apulia region.) However, Merz bars entry to his shelter with razor-sharp edges and metal projections. The conspicuous staples, bolts, and clamps suggest an industrial mode of construction. In the late 60s, Merz was a member of *Arte Povera*, or "poor art," a group of artists who made the decision to work with cheap, everyday materials, partly as a political gesture.

LIFE DEATH
Bruce Nauman; 1983; 37 in (94 cm) diameter; neon
In his work, Bruce Nauman (b. 1941) uses the loud, commercial qualities of brightly colored neon tubing, which is so evocative of street signs and advertising, to offset the mystery and truth of language. By using words of either similar sound or form or, as here, contradictory meaning, he challenges his viewer to reject logical thinking. His flashing lights put the power back into cliché and monumentalize a play on words.

PLASTIC PALETTE II
Tony Cragg; 1985;
5¼ x 5½ ft (1.75 x 1.7 m); plastic
Like a modern archaeologist, Tony Cragg (b. 1929) collects fragments of colored plastic and sorts them into categories by color and shape – piecing together a picture of our society. The seductive, bright, figurative forms entice the viewer into appreciating the man-made, inorganic world, which can be just as beautiful as the organic and natural one. By making the origins of each object apparent, Cragg challenges traditional art.

JUNKYARD
As gathering places for household rubbish, junkyards testify to the social values of a particular area and even society at large. For this reason, modern artists have realized their potential as a source for materials and inspiration.

CAR DOOR, IRONING BOARD AND TWIN-TUB WITH NORTH AMERICAN INDIAN HEAD-DRESS
Bill Woodrow; 1981
Bill Woodrow (b. 1948) creates his sculptures by slicing, cutting, and bending the skins of discarded household objects. The various items are tied together by an "umbilical cord"; here, he has used a cutout from the washing machine. Though his work tends toward the comically naive, it also offers revelations about our throwaway society. The introduction of an Indian headdress, for instance, among the rubbish of Western "civilization" works as a reminder of more ancient and dignified cultures.

The cutout cord, which originates with the washing machine, appears to terminate in the lawn mower

The "site specific"

ALTHOUGH SCULPTORS have always sought inspiration from nature and the outside world, it is only in the 20th century that they have begun to work directly with their surroundings. The desire to make art more accessible and to remove it from the intimidating atmosphere of galleries and museums has led artists to place more importance on the environment in which a piece is positioned. In "site specific" sculptures, the setting becomes the foremost consideration for the artist, influencing form and meaning. The intention is to involve the viewer to a greater extent, and in some outdoor pieces even to provoke the most elemental reactions to the natural landscape. Richard Long (b. 1945) manipulates the land to his own desires, while Christo Javaceff (b. 1935) wraps or curtains off areas. The late Joseph Beuys (1921–86) made a bid to escape the corruption of civilization and the art world by creating a new, secure world through installation and performance. Most of the works shown here are temporary and exist in the long term only through photographs.

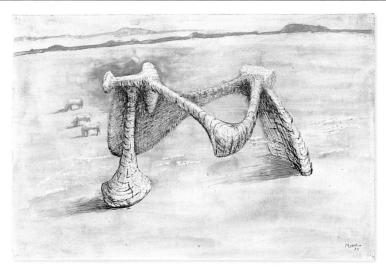

SCULPTURAL OBJECT IN LANDSCAPE
Henry Moore; 1939; watercolor and pen
For Henry Moore (p. 54), the landscape was a major source of energy and interest. As this sketch of an idea for a sculpture shows, he preempted the interest of today's sculptors in the site specific. Here, his inclusion of hills and grazing sheep are integral to his invention of a sculptural form. Moore intended many of his finished works to be shown in natural settings, where the sky would form the backdrop and there could be no distractions from the other art objects that are generally present in galleries.

SLOW MOVEMENT
Anthony Caro; 1965; 57 x 118 x 24 in
(145 x 300 x 61 cm); painted steel
Here, Anthony Caro (b. 1924) uses industrial metals, which are evidently welded together, in a natural setting. When placed directly on the ground, the work echoes the lines of path and fence. While our eye is guided along the path by the fence and steel projections, progress along the path is barred. Both title and form refer to the viewer's relationship with the landscape.

WALKING A LINE IN PERU
Richard Long; 1972; 25 x 34½ in (64 x 87.5 cm); photograph and text on board
In his sculptures, Richard Long attempts to make direct marks on the landscape with the minimal amount of intervention necessary: as temporary structures their existence has no lasting effect. Using the land as his only resource, like a Stone Age sculptor (pp. 8–9), he moves his natural materials to his chosen site. This photograph shows a line of stones that Long laid down during a walk across Peru. Its straight, vertical form bisects some curvy ground markings, which were made by the native Nazca people of the region some two thousand years ago.

SPIRAL JETTY
Robert Smithson; 1970;
1500 x 15 ft (457 x 4.6 m); stone
Removing earth from one site to another, Smithson made a number of "site/nonsite" works. The form of this spiral is influenced by archaic sculptures (p. 9), which similarly can only be seen in full from the sky.

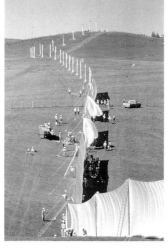

CHRISTO AND JEANNE-CLAUDE CHRISTO

The *Running Fence* took four years from idea to realization, 18 public hearings, three court sessions, the cooperation of 59 ranch owners, and a 450-page environmental report – making good organization necessary at every stage. Unlike studio-based artists, this husband-and-wife team has to organize and supervise engineers, assistants, occasional helpers, and spectators, while maintaining their creative energies and the insight to realize the possibilities and restrictions of each project.

THE RUNNING FENCE
Christo; 1972–6; 18 ft x 24½ miles (5.5 m x 39 km); cloth
Here, the *Running Fence* is shown during various stages of its construction and at its completion (bottom right). Ending at the Pacific Ocean, the white nylon curtain was made to stretch across 24 miles of California countryside. Although 65 full-time workers were employed for two months to install the poles, 360 students were also called in for two weeks just to hang the curtain. Unlike most barriers, this fence was not made to be defensive or protective, but to respond directly to the shifting pattern of natural light.

Felt rolls insulate the entire installation, creating an atmosphere of safety

PLIGHT (DETAIL)
Joseph Beuys; 1958–85; felt, piano, blackboard, and thermometer
Believing that exhibition space is not mere housing, Beuys made his installation works specifically for the gallery. During World War II, he was shot down as a fighter pilot and was saved by nomadic Tartars, who, in order to keep him warm, smeared him with fat and wrapped him in felt. He constantly refers back to this wartime experience: using these references to protection and survival, Beuys encases the gallery with felt and raw wool, capitalizing on the emotive effects and physical sensations caused by the overwhelming smell, deadened sound, stifling warmth, and claustrophobic conditions. He displays his instinct for these qualities by submerging the viewer in a womblike atmosphere that stimulates all five of the senses.

Glossary

Abrasive Sand or powdered pumice stone, which is rubbed against a sculpture's surface to create a smooth and polished effect.

Abstract A term that can be employed to describe any art that does not represent recognizable objects. In the 20th century, it has been applied to works that use color and form to convey particular ideas or theories.

Abstract Expressionism The nongeometric abstract art movement that flourished in America after the Second World War.

Adze A cutting tool used by woodcarvers to rough out the basic form of a work. Though its blade is generally steel, in pre-Bronze Age cultures it was stone.

Alabaster A soft, translucent stone that is easily cut and carved. Prone to scratching and deterioration, it is unsuitable for outdoor pieces.

Armature A metal skeletal support, over which clay or wax is modeled.

Bronze An alloy of approximately 90 percent copper and 10 percent tin, which contains small amounts of other metals such as lead or zinc. Hard and durable, it is workable both hot and cold, making it ideally suited to casting (pp. 26–27).

Brass An alloy of copper and zinc that is malleable and stronger than copper.

Calliper A measuring instrument that has two parallel jaws – one fixed and the other sliding.

Capital An architectural term for the upper part of a column or pier.

Carving A traditional subtractive method of producing a sculpture in which the material is cut or chipped away.

Cast A work produced with a mold.

Chasing The final process of finishing a bronze cast once it has cooled from the furnace (see p. 27). Chisels and punches are used to remove imperfections and holes and to create fine detail. The surface is polished and smoothed down.

Junkyards are a source of material for modern sculptors

Chisel A steel tool used for shaping wood, stone, or metal. It has to be held at an angle and struck with a mallet to force the sharp cutting edge along the surface of a carving. In the ordinary chisel this cutting edge is straight (see claw chisel).

Classical Though this label is most often applied to the style of art initially developed by the ancient Greeks and Romans, it can also be employed to describe any period in a culture's history that is characterized by emotional restraint and conservatism, e.g., Classic Maya art (p. 12).

A claw chisel with pointed prongs

Claw chisel Unlike the ordinary chisel (see chisel), it has a cutting edge divided into two or more prongs. For working marble, each prong is pointed (as above), whereas for stone each claw is flat.

Clay A malleable, moist earth mixed with water that becomes hard when baked. Popularly used by sculptors for modeling (pp. 34–35).

Commission A work that is produced to a buyer's requirements and specifications.

Composition The considered arrangement of the various parts of a work of art.

Contrapposto A classical pose that most often occurs in figures of male nudes. The body weight is concentrated on one leg so that the torso is twisted and the hips are pointed in the opposite direction from the head and shoulders.

Drill A mechanical tool used for boring holes by means of a revolving cutting point.

Earthenware Clay pieces or vessels that have been baked hard.

Emery A grayish black mineral used as an abrasive for smoothing and polishing stone.

Figurative Art in which figures or objects are portrayed.

Glaze A mixture of oxidized tin,

lead, and fine sand, which is combined with pigment to give terra-cotta a colored surface that is both tough and impermeable.

Grog Pulverized brick or pottery that is mixed with plaster during the lost-wax process to create the core for the bronze cast (pp. 26–27).

Lacquer A clear resin, which can be colored. Applied in layers, it seals and protects an object.

Limestone A type of marble that is softer and easier to work than a more crystalline stone.

Demon and a Lady of Rank, Chartres Cathedral

Lost-wax process The system of making a bronze cast in which metal replaces a wax model in the mold so that it melts away and is "lost" (see pp. 26–27).

Maquette A small model that is used by sculptors to make preliminary sketches.

Marble A hard, crystalline stone, capable of taking fine detailing and high polish. It is available in a spectrum of colors (see pp. 38–39).

Minimalism A modern art movement that emerged in the United States during the 1950s, when sculptors started focusing on the most elemental geometric forms (pp. 56–57).

Mobile A form of sculpture that was created by Calder in 1932. Generally made out of shapes of color connected by wires, it moves freely in the air, creating three-dimensional movement (pp. 56–57).

Mold A hollow shape that takes the negative form of a sculpture that is to be cast.

Molding A decorative strip or edge, traditionally carved or molded.

Nephrite A form of jade.

Patron Someone who financially

supports an artist, either directly, by providing them with a salary, or indirectly, by buying their work.

Pigments Substances used as a coloring agent; pigments were originally made from natural products. In the 20th century, the range of hues was vastly increased with the development of synthetic colors.

A marble quarry at Carrara, in Italy

Plaster A fine powder – made from the mineral gypsum. When mixed with water it forms a quick-setting paste. It is used by sculptors for casts and models.

Plinth A block, made of wood or stone that raises a sculpture up off the ground.

Plumb line A string with a metal weight at one end that is used to determine verticality.

Porcelain The finest of all ceramics, porcelain retains its strength even when it is very thin.

Proportion The correct or desirable relationship between parts.

Punch A pointed steel tool used like a chisel to remove chips or stone.

Rasp A steel tool with sharp raised points (similar to a cheese grater). The points, which range from fine to coarse, are used to smooth the surface of a sculpture.

Relief A term for sculptures with a flat background. The forms and lines of the image can either project from the surface or be incised into it.

Rubbing stone A shaped stone, used to smooth a sculpture's surface.

Sandstone A porous, soft stone.

Schematic A simple, generalized depiction of a subject.

Slip A mixture of clay and water, to which pigment is added, to decorate the surface of ceramic items.

Clay modeling tools

Softwood Wood from conifers – pines and firs – which is softer and less durable than hardwood.

Soldering A method of joining two pieces of metal together with a different metal that has a lower melting point.

Sculpture collections

The following shows the locations of sculpture collections, worldwide, that have works featured in this book.

EUROPE
Austria
Vienna Kunsthistorisches Museum

France
Paris Musée du Louvre; Musée d'Orsay; Musée Rodin

Germany
Berlin Staatliche Museen
Bonn Rheinisches Landesmuseum
Munich Neue Pinakothek

Greece
Athens Acropolis Museum; National Museum

Italy
Florence Bargello; Accademia
Rome Galleria Borghese, Museo Pio-Clementino, Vatican

Switzerland
Zurich Museum Reitberg

U.K.
London British Museum; Tate Gallery; Victoria & Albert Museum
Norwich Sainsbury Centre for Visual Arts, University of East Anglia

NORTH AMERICA
Canada
Vancouver University of British Columbia

ASIA
Japan
Tokyo Collection Galerie Tokoro

AFRICA
Nigeria
Lagos National Museum

Works on display

The following is a list of locations where the sculptures reproduced in this book can be found.

Key: *t*=top, *b*=bottom, *l*=left, *r*=right, *c*=center

Abbreviations
B: Bargello, Florence, Italy; **BM**: British Museum, London; **ML**: Musée du Louvre, Paris; **SCVA**: Sainsbury Centre for Visual Arts, University of East Anglia, Norwich, England; **TG**: Tate Gallery, London; **V&A**: Victoria & Albert Museum, London.

p. 6 l: *Figure of Ku*, Museum of Mankind, London; bc: *Netsuke*, BM; c: *Nok Head*, National Museum, Lagos; br: *Demon and a Lady of Rank*, Chartres Cathedral, France.

p. 7 tc: *Appennine*, Villa Demidoff, Pratolino, Italy; cl: *Three Graces* (model for), Gipsoteca, Possagno, Italy; r: *Monument for V. Tatlin*, TG; bc: *Linear Construction No. 2*, TG.

p. 8 tl: *Venus of Willendorf*, University Museum of Archaeology and Anthropology, Cambridge, England; b: *Stonehenge*, Salisbury Plain, England.

p. 9 cl: *Mammoth*, University Museum of Archaeology and Anthropology, Cambridge; tr: *Candelabra*, Paracas, Peru; bc: *Bison*, Tuc d'Audoubert, Ariége, France; br: *Female Idol with Arms Folded*, SCVA

p. 10 tr: *Neck Pendant*, SCVA; bl: *Baby Carrier*, SCVA.

p. 11 tr: *Ladle*, SCVA; tl: *Ivory Head*, SCVA; cr: *Polar Bear*, private collection; b: *Drill Bow*, SCVA

p. 12 tl: *Crystal Skull*, BM; tr: *Miniature Stele*, SCVA; bl: *Smiling Face*, SCVA; *Conch Shell*, SCVA.

p. 13 tl: *Turquoise Mask*, Museum of Mankind, London; tr: *Pyramid of Magician*, Uxmal, Mexico; b: *The Nunnery*, Uxmal, Mexico; cl: *Chacmool*, El Templo Mayor Site, Mexico.

p. 14 tl: *Crown*, SCVA; tr: *Head*, SCVA; bl: *Ritual Figure*, SCVA; br: *Divination Cup*, SCVA.

p. 15 tr: *Horseman*, SCVA; cr: *Cow Mask*, SCVA; bl: *Head of an Oba*, SCVA.

p. 16 l: *Tomb Figure*, SCVA; br: *Terracotta Army*, Quin Shi Huang Di's Tomb, Xian, China; cr: *Sacred General*, Buddhist Temple, To-ji, Japan.

p. 17 r: *Shiva Nataraja*, Museum Reitberg, Zurich; bl, br: Buddhist Temple at Borobudur, Central Java, Indonesia.

p. 18 bl: *Hole in the Sky*, Kitwancool, Skeena River, British Columbia, Canada.

p. 20 bl: *Cat*, ML; cr: *Temple of King Rameses II*, Abu Simbel, Egypt; bl: *The Giza Sphinx*, Giza, Egypt; br: *Marching Hippopotamus*, SCVA.

p. 21 r: *Standing Couple*, ML; bl: *The Seated Scribe*, ML.

p. 22 bl: *Kouros*, National Museum, Athens; bc: *Kritian Boy*, Acropolis Museum, Athens; br: *Discus Thrower*, Museo delle Terme, Rome.

p. 23 tl: *The Parthenon Frieze*, BM; r: *Caryatid*, BM; cl: *Head of Sophocles*, BM.

p. 24 tl: *Head of Claudius*, location unknown; cl: *Mourning Woman*, BM; bc: *Laocoön*, Museo Pio-Clementino, Vatican, Rome; br: *Augustus*, Braccio Nuovo, Vatican.

p. 25 t: *Trajan's Column*, Via dei Fori Imperiali, Rome; bl: *Bronze Horses*, Piazza San Marco, Venice.

p. 26 tr: *The Pireus Apollo*, National Museum, Athens; bl: *Marcus Aurelius*, Piazza del Campidoglio, Rome.

p. 27 b: Six stages of bronze casting, V&A; cr: *Gattamelata*; Piazza del Santo, Padua, Italy.

p. 28 tl: *Male portrait from Ephesus*, Kunsthistorisches Museum, Vienna; c: *North Cross*, East Face Ahenny, Co. Tipperary, Ireland; cr: *Prophet Isaiah*, Portal at Souillac, Périgord, France; bl: *Harbaville Triptych*, ML.

p. 29 l: *Madonna of Kruman*, Kunsthistorisches Museum, Vienna; tr: *Vesper Image*, Rheinisches Landesmuseum, Bonn; br: *Group Attending Crucifixion*, SCVA.

pp. 30–31 Sculptures from Chartres Cathedral, Chartres, Loire, France.

p. 32 cl: *Sacrifice of Isaac* (Ghiberti), B; bl: *Hercules and Antaeus*, B; br: *Sacrifice of Isaac* (Brunelleschi), B.

p. 33 tl: *Feast of Herod*, Siena Baptistery Font, Siena Italy; bl: *David*; B; c: *Marzocco Lion*, B; br: *David*, B.

p. 34 bl: *Madonna and Child*, B; br: *The Madonna and Laughing Child*, V&A

p. 35 tr: *St. John the Evangelist*, Pazzi Chapel, Sta. Croce, Florence.

p. 36 tl: *Rondanini Pietà*, Castello Sforzesco, Milan; br: *Pietà*, St. Peters, Rome.

p. 37 br: *David*, Accademia, Florence.

p. 38 bl: *Apollo and Daphne*, Galleria Borghese, Rome

p. 39 l: *Pitti Tondo*, B; tr: *The Awakening Slave*, Accademia, Florence

p. 40 l: *Rape of the Sabine Women*, Loggia dei Lanzi, Florence; br: *Salt Cellar*, Kunsthistorisches Museum, Vienna.

p. 41 l: *Perseus*, Loggia dei Lanzi, Florence.

p. 42 *The Ecstacy of St. Teresa*, Cornaro Chapel, Sta. Maria della Vittoria, Rome.

p. 43 tl: *The Dragon Fountain*, Palace of Versailles, Paris; tr: *Atlantean Caryatids*, Upper Belvedere, Vienna; br: *The Great Elector*, Schloß Charlottenberg, Berlin.

p. 44 b: *Four Rivers Fountain*, Piazza Navona, Rome.

p. 45 tl: *Plague Column*, Graben, Vienna; tr: *Porch of San Telmo*, San Telmo, Seville, Spain; b: *Mexico City Cathedral*, Mexico

p. 46 tr: *Denis Diderot*, ML; bl: *Monument to the Princesses . . .*, Staatliche Museen, Berlin; br: *Menacing Cupid*, ML.

p. 47 tl: *The Three Graces* (model), Gipsoteca, Passagno, Italy; br: Monument to Viscountess Fitzharris, Christchurch Priory, Hampshire.

p. 48 l: *Statue of Liberty*, New York; tr: *Arch of Triumph*, Place Charles de Gaulle, Paris; br: *Eros*, Piccadilly Circus, London.

p. 49 tl: *Royal Artillery Monument*, Hyde Park Corner, London; r: *Worker and the Collective Farm Girl*, Exhibition of Economic Achievements of the U.S.S.R., Moscow; bl: *St. Louis Gateway Arch*, St. Louis, Missouri.

p. 50 *The Kiss*, TG.

p. 51 tl: *The Age of Bronze*, TG; tc: *The Crouching Woman*, TG; r: *Monument to Balzac*, Musée Rodin, Paris; bl: *Dancer*, Musée d'Orsay, Paris; bc: *Little Dancer Aged 14*, S.C.V.A.

p. 52 bl: *Rock Drill*, TG; cr: *The Kiss*, Musée National d'Art Moderne, Paris.

p. 53 tl: *Guitar*, Musée Picasso, Paris; tr: *Fountain*, Collection Galerie Tokoro, Tokyo; bl: *Head No. 2*, TG; br: *Lobster Telephone*, TG.

p. 54 l: *The Bird*, Musée National d'Art Moderne, Paris; lc: *Oval Sculpture No. 2*, TG; rc: *Mother and Child*, S.C.V.A.; br: *Maquette for Madonna and Child*, TG.

p. 55 tl: *Forms on a Bow*, TG; bl: *Woman*, S.C.V.A.; r: *Horseman*, TG.

p. 56 bl: *Cubi XIX*, TG; c: *Antennae with Red and Blue Dots*, TG.

p. 57 c: *Bi Cd in Contrail*, private collection; tr: *Running Arcs for John Cage*, Kunst Sammlung Nordrhein-Westfalen, Germany; bl: *Untitled*, TG.

p. 58 tl: *Puppy*, temporary installation; cr: *Do We Turn Round Inside Houses or Is It Houses Which Turn Around Us?*, TG; bl: *Life Death*, private collection.

p. 59 b: *Car Door, Ironing Board and Twin-Tub with North American Indian Head-Dress*, TG; tc: *Plastic Palette II*, private collection.

p. 60 cr: *Slow Movement*, Arts Council Collection, Britain. The other works on this and the following page were temporary and exist now only through photographs.

Index

Acknowledgments

PICTURE CREDITS
Every effort has been made to trace the copyright holders and we apologize in advance for any unintentional omissions. We would be pleased to insert the appropriate acknowledgment in any subsequent edition of this publication.
Key: *t*: top *b*: bottom *c*: center *l*: left *r*: right
Abbreviations: AA: Ancient Art and Architecture Collection; **BAL:** Bridgeman Art Library; **BM:** Trustees of the British Museum, London; **ML:** Musée du Louvre, Paris; **RMN:** Réunion des Musées Nationaux, Paris; **SC:** Scala; **SCVA:** Robert and Lisa Sainsbury Collection, Sainsbury Centre for Visual Arts, University of East Anglia, Norwich/Photo: James Austin; **TS:** Tate Gallery, London; **TS:** Tony Stone; **V&A:** Courtesy of the Board of Trustees of the Victoria & Albert Museum, London; **WF:** Werner Forman Archive
Front cover: Clockwise from top left: SCVA; Courtesy of Lyle Wilson and the University of British Columbia Museum of Anthropology, Vancouver/Photo Bill McLennan; Bargello, Florence/SC; TG; TG; Museo delle Terme, Rome/SC; SCVA; TG; University Museum of Archaeology and Anthropology, Cambridge
Back cover: SCVA; TS; BM; SCVA; V&A; ML/RMN; Bargello, Florence/SC; Gipsoteca, Possagno/SC **Inside front flap:** AA; Museo Pio-Clementino, Vatican, Rome/SC
p1: SCVA **p2:** *tl:* Biblioteca Medicea Laurenziana, Florence; *tc:* SCVA/© ADAGP, Paris and DACS, London 1994; *bl:* SCVA/© The Henry Moore Foundation; *br:* SCVA; *tr:* Towneley Hall Art Gallery, Burnley/BAL; *c:* Mary Evans Picture Library; *bcr:* TS **p3:** *l:* SCVA; *c:* TG/© Bill Woodrow; *r:* Baptistry, Siena Cathedral/SC **p4:** *tl:* TG; *tc:* Musée d'Orsay, Paris; *tr, bc, br:* SCVA; *bl:* Galleria Borghese, Rome/SC **p5:** *br:* SCVA **p6:** *l:* BM; *c:* AA; *br:* © Sonia Halliday Photographs **p7:** *tc:* Villa Demidoff, Pratolino/SC; *cl:* Gipsoteca, Possagno/SC; *r:* TG/© 1994 Dan Flavin/ARS, New York; *bc:* TG/© Nina Williams **p8:** *tl:* University Museum of Archaeology and Anthropology, Cambridge **pp8-9:** *b:* A. F. Kersting **p9:** *tl:* University Museum of Archaeology and Anthropology, Cambridge; *tr:* Nick Saunders/Barbara Heller; *bc:* AA; *br:* SCVA **p10:** *tr, bl:* SCVA **p11:** *tr, tl, b:* SCVA; *cr:* WF; *cl:* Canadian Museum of Civilisation, negative # 39707 **p12:** *tl:* BM; *tr, bl, br:* SCVA **p13:** *tl:* AA; *tr, b:* WF; *cl:* Nick Saunders/Barbara Heller **p14:** *tl, tr, bl, bc, br:* SCVA **p15:** *tr:* BM; *cr, bl:* SCVA **p16:** *l:* SCVA; *c, br:* TS; *cr:* WF **p17:** *r:* Edward van der Heydt Collection, Museum Reitberg, Zurich/Photo: Wettstein & Kauf; *bl, br:* WF **p18:** *ts:* Heather Angel; *bl:* WF; *cr:* Canadian Museum of Civilisation, negative # 255 **p19:** *t:* Courtesy of Lyle Wilson and the University of British Columbia Museum of Anthropology, Vancouver/Photo: Bill McLennan; *b:* Courtesy of the artists, Stan Bevan and Ken McNeil/Photo: Bill McLennan **p20:** *tl:* ML/RMN; *cr:* Courtesy of George Hart, Education Department, BM; *bl:* WF; *br:* SCVA **p21:** *tl:* BM; *tc:* Mary Evans Picture Library; *r, bl:* RMN **p22:** *tr (detail): The Acropolis, Athens*, Leo von Klenze, Neue Pinakothek, München/Artothek; *bl:* National Museum, Athens/SC; *br:* Museo delle Terme, Rome/SC **p23:** *tl, r:* BM; *cl:* AA **p24:** *tl:* AA; *cl:* BM; *bc:* Museo Pio-Clementino, Vatican, Rome/SC; *br:* Braccio Nuovo, Vatican, Rome/SC **p25:** *tl, tr, br:* SC; *bl:* S. Marco, Venice/SC **p26:** *tl:* V&A; *tr:* National Museum, Athens/SC; *bl:* Piazza del Campidoglio, Rome/SC **pp26-27:** *b:* V&A **p27:** *t, cl:* from Diderot and Alembert's *L'Encyclopedie*, Vol. 8, Paris, 1771; *cr:* Piazza del Santo, Padua/SC **p28:** *l:* Kunsthistorisches Museum, Vienna; *cr:* Office of Public Works, Ireland; *br:* Giraudon; *bl:* ML/RMN **p29:** *l:* Kunsthistorisches Museum, Vienna; *tr:* Rheinisches Landesmuseum, Bonn; *br:* SCVA **p30:** *tl, cr:* © Sonia Halliday Photographs; *cl, bc:* © Sonia Halliday and Laura Lushington **p31:** *tl, tr, bc, br:* © Sonia Halliday and Laura Lushington; *c:* © Sonia Halliday Photographs **p32:** *cl, bl, br:* Bargello, Florence/SC **p33:** *tl:* Baptistry, Siena Cathedral/SC; *tr:* Campo SS. Giovanni e Paolo, Venice/SC; *bl, c, br:* Bargello, Florence/SC **p34:** *tl, br:* V&A; *bl:* Bargello, Florence/SC **p35:** *tr, br:* Pazzi Chapel, Sta. Croce, Florence/SC **p36:** *tl:* Castello Sforzesco, Milan/SC; *bl:* Ashmolean Museum, Oxford; *br:* S. Pietro, Rome/SC **p37:** *l:* ML/SCALA; *tr:* SC; *c:* Reproduced by courtesy of the Trustees, the National Gallery, London; *bc:* V&A; *br:* Accademia, Florence/SC **p38:** *tl:* Galleria Borghese, Rome/SC; *bc:* Private Collection, from *The Artist's Craft*, James Ayres, Phaidon Press Ltd, 1985 **p39:** *l, br (details):* Bargello, Florence/SC; *tr:* Accademia, Florence/SC **p40:** *l, cl (detail):* Loggia dei Lanzi, Florence/SC; *tr:* Kunsthistorisches Museum, Vienna/BAL **p41:** *l, br, tc (detail):* Loggia dei Lanzi, Florence/SC; *cr:* Biblioteca Laurenziana, Florence **p42:** *tl, r (detail):* Sta. Maria della Vittoria, Rome/SC **p43:** *tl:* Caisse Nationale des Monuments Historiques et des Sites/© DACS 1994; *tr:* Wim Swaan; *cl:* Bibliothèque Nationale, Paris; *br:* Schloß Charlottenburg, Berlin/Bildarchiv Preussischer Kulturbesitz **p44:** *tl:* Architectural Association/Photo: David Hertzig; *cl:* TS; *b, cr:* Piazza Navona, Rome/SC **p45:** *tr:* © Firo-Foto, Barcelona; *bl:* © Andes Press Agency/Photo: Carlos Reyes **p46:** *tl:* Mary Evans Picture Library; *tr:* ML/Giraudon/BAL; *bl:* Staatliche Museen zu Berlin, Preussischer Kulturbesitz, Nationalgalerie/Photo: Klaus Göken, 1992; *cr:* Jean-Loup Charmet, Paris; *br:* ML/RMN **p47:** *tl:* Gipsoteca, Possagno/SC; *tr:* Towneley Hall Art Gallery, Burnley/BAL; *cr:* from *Anatomia per uso dei pittori e scultori*, Rome, 1811; *bl:* from *The Artist's Craft*, James Ayres, Phaidon Press Ltd, 1985; *br:* Christchurch Priory, Hampshire **p48:** *l:* TS; *tr:* The Fine Art Society/BAL **p49:** *tl, c (detail):* Hyde Park, London; *r:* © Mark Wadlow, Russia & Republics Photo Library, Middlesex; *bl:* TS **p50:** *l:* Musée Rodin, Paris; *b:* TG **p51:** *tl, tc:* V&A/On loan to the Tate Gallery, London; *c:* Musée Rodin, Paris; *r:* Musée Rodin, Paris/Photo: Bruno Jarret/© ADAGP, Paris and DACS, London 1994; *bc:* SCVA **p52:** *tl:* © Roger-Viollet; *bl:* TG; *cr:* Musée Nationale d'Art Moderne, Paris/Lauros-Giraudon/BAL/© ADAGP, Paris and DACS, London 1994 **p53:** *t:* Musée Picasso/RMN/© DACS 1994; *tr:* Collection Galerie Tokoro, Tokyo/© ADAGP, Paris and DACS, London 1994; *bl:* TG/© Nina Williams; *br:* TG/© DEMART PRO ARTE BV/DACS 1994 **p54:** *l:* Musée Nationale d'Art Moderne/Lauros-Giraudon/© ADAGP, Paris and DACS, London 1994; *tr:* The Hulton Deutsch Collection; *lc:* TG; *br:* TG/© Reproduced by permission of The Henry Moore Foundation; *rc:* SCVA/© Reproduced by permission of The Henry Moore Foundation **p55:** *tl:* TG/© Sir Eduardo Paolozzi; *c:* TG/© ADAGP, Paris and DACS, London 1994; *r:* TG/© DACS 1994 **p56:** *bl:* TG/© David Smith/DACS, London and VAGA, New York/Photo: Philippe Halsman **pp56–57:** *c:* TG/© ADAGP, Paris and DACS, London 1994 **p57:** *c:* Anthony d'Offay Gallery, London/© Carl Andre/DACS, London and VAGA, New York 1994; *tr:* Installed Kunst Sammlung Nordrhein-Westfalen/Photo: Erika Kiffl, Düsseldorf/© 1993 Richard Serra/ARS, New York; *bl:* TG **p58:** *tl:* © Jeff Koons; *cr:* TG; *bl:* Courtesy of the Leo Castelli Gallery, New York/© 1993 Bruce Nauman/ARS, New York **pp58-59:** TG/© Bill Woodrow; *tc:* Courtesy Lisson Gallery, London; *cr:* Astrid & Hanns-Frieder Michler/Science Photo Library, London **p60:** *tr:* SCVA/© Reproduced by permission of The Henry Moore Foundation; *bl:* photo: Stephen White, courtesy Lisson Gallery, London; *cr:* Arts Council Collection/Photo: John Goldblatt/© Sir Anthony Caro; *br:* Gianfranco Gorgoni, New York **p61:** Photo © Wolfgang Volz 1988; *tc, tr, tcr, cr:* © Christo 1976/Photo: Wolfgang Volz; *bl:* Anthony d'Offay Gallery, London/© DACS 1994 **p62:** *c:* © Sonia Halliday Photographs; *bl:* Astrid & Hanns-Frieder Michler Science Photo Library, London
Additional Photography: Max Alexander: p48: *tr;* Andy Crawford: p49: *tl, cl;* John Heseltine: p48: *tl, c, br;* p2: *tcr;* p62: *cr;* Dave King: p8: *tl;* p9: *tl;* Neil Lukas: p43: *tl;* David Miller: p47: *br;* Nick Nicholls: p23: *tl;* Karen Shapiro: p32: *tl;* Philippe Sebert: p4: *tc;* p51: *bl;* Peter Wilson: p45: *tl*
Artworks: Sallie Alane Reason: p15: *tl;* p23: *bl*
Dorling Kindersley would like to thank: Kate Carreno and Kay Poludniowski at the Sainsbury Centre for Visual Arts, who organized the photographic shoot and supplied us with so much information about the objects in the collection; Joanne Pillsbury, for checking the non-Western section of the book so stringently; Liz Wilkinson, who enabled us to benefit from her expertise in Far Eastern sculpture; Sonia Halliday, for allowing us to use her wonderful photographs of Chartres; Clayman, West Sussex, who provided us with terra-cotta tiles and pigments; and Jeanne-Claude and Christo, who were forever helpful and enthusiastic. Thanks are also due to the following members of the Eyewitness Art Team: Toni Kay, Simon Murrell, and Sean Moore; a special thank you goes to the picture researchers, Jo Evans, Julia Harris-Voss, and Jo Walton, who gave their unerring support throughout; and, Lauren Brown, Gwen Edmonds, and Peter Jones, all deserve an additional thank you for the care that they took in checking and commenting on the text.
Author's acknowledgments:
I would like to thank all my family for their constant support throughout this project; with a special thanks to my partner Keith for his endless patience and interest. Many thanks to all at Dorling Kindersley, and an additional thanks to Helen Castle, Liz Brown, and Peter Jones. A very small thanks to Emma the dog, who hindered my every move.